SECOND THRESHOLD

3 - 35

Miranda.

I tell you I won't have it
that way!

Josiah.

Why not? — Not the world or
his things to blame for it, mind
you. — himself, and himself
only. Arrived at last! Himself destroyed and his daughter
set by him firmly on the
path ~~by him~~ to the same
end... A fine, crowning
achievement to a lifelong
struggle, eh? What do you
say? I say, let him rot. —
Go on — clear out now, both of
you. Leave me alone.

Miranda.

No. We'll not! We'll never!

Josiah.

Don't be fearful any more, daughter.
Something else goes in the
process: courage. I'm likely to

A page of Philip Barry's manuscript for the
final scene of *Second Threshold*.

SECOND
THRESHOLD

by

PHILIP BARRY

WITH REVISIONS AND A PREFACE BY
ROBERT E. SHERWOOD

HARPER & BROTHERS PUBLISHERS
New York

SECOND THRESHOLD

Preface

By Robert Sherwood

My first encounter with Philip Barry was not of a nature to suggest the beginning of a beautiful friendship. It was in the spring of 1921. We were both twenty-five years old and had seen service overseas in the First World War. Both of us were leading a hand-to-mouth existence. He was a postgraduate student of playwriting in Professor George Pierce Baker's English 47 Workshop at Harvard, but he was also working for an advertising agency in order to support himself through another year of the Baker course. I was a movie critic and associate editor on *Life* (at that time a humorous magazine, at least nominally).

I had received a letter from a Harvard classmate of mine, James Seymour, who was an assistant of Professor Baker's. He wrote that the Workshop was producing a play, *A Punch for Judy*, by one of the students, Philip Barry; it was planned to give performances of this play in New York and other eastern cities during the Easter vacation; and would I help them to get some publicity? I wrote Seymour that I'd be glad to do all I could and so would my colleague on *Life*, Robert Benchley, another Harvard man and one who had already achieved celebrity as a critic and a major wit. Benchley and I knew most of the dramatic critics and editors of the time—including Heywood Broun, Alexander Woollcott, George S. Kaufman, Ward Morehouse—and we managed to obtain much more publicity for this amateur performance than would ordinarily have been the case.

However, when the Baker troupe arrived in New York, Seymour telephoned to say that Barry wanted to have a talk with Benchley and me, so we arranged a meeting at lunch at the Harvard Club. When Seymour had performed the introductions, Barry looked at us and said, "I understand you two have been handling the publicity." Benchley said, diffidently, that we had done our best. Barry said, coldly, "Well, it hasn't been any good." He told us that he was highly dissatisfied with our work (for which, of course, we had not been paid). He berated us for undertaking a job for which we were obviously not qualified.

As Benchley and I walked along 44th Street toward the Fifth Avenue bus after this session, we were muttering imprecations about this "precocious, presumptuous, exasperating young twirp."

So—both Benchley and I eventually became devoted and admiring friends of Phil Barry.

That first play of his, *A Punch for Judy*, was presented in 1921 at the same Morosco Theatre where his last play, *Second Threshold*, is now playing as I write this, thirty years later. As a footnote: in the original cast of *A Punch for Judy* was another of Baker's students, a young hopeful named John Mason Brown, who subsequently abandoned his acting career to the immeasurable gain of dramatic criticism and the lecture platform.

I cannot pretend to write a critical analysis of Phil Barry's career or evaluation of the twenty or more plays that he left behind him. Five years after *A Punch for Judy* I wrote my first play, *The Road to Rome*, and after that Barry and I became in a sense competitors. Professional jealousy is no less prevalent among playwrights than it is in other professions or arts; it may well be more so, because in the theater the dividing line between success and failure is so horribly distinct and decisive, and those on the wrong side of the line are apt to look with envy and resentment at fortune's favorites (or maybe the more talented) across the border. It happened that in four years, 1927-1931, when I tasted only failure, Barry was writing one big hit after another: *Paris Bound, Holiday, Tomorrow and Tomorrow, The Animal Kingdom.* Then our positions were completely reversed: years went by when I had nothing but bewildering success and he had nothing but bewildering discouragement. However, we managed to remain friends. I respected him as an artist. Once, in another preface to another play, I wrote that the American writer is inclined to be ashamed and mortified if anyone inadvertently applies the term "artist" to him—that he fears there is some sissy connotation in that word; but Barry had no such fears. As an artist he wrote, and as an artist he lived. The capacity for exasperation which had so irritated Benchley and me when we first met him was always part of him, as was the tremendous capacity for love. I also respected him as a worker, but I never really appreciated the extent of his industriousness until I myself became involved, after his sudden death, in the final processes of bringing *Second Threshold* to the stage.

I learned that he had spent at least eleven years on this play, developing its theme, its characters, its essential story in his restless mind. He wrote four complete drafts of it in his last years. In the final days of his life he wrote the play's finest scene, the breast-baring, soul-searching confessional by Josiah which comes near the end. A page from this scene, the last writing that Philip Barry ever did, is reproduced elsewhere in this book.

The first known note on *Second Threshold* is as follows:

Daughter

The man of 42 at the end of his soul's rope, recovering from attempt at suicide.

The daughter he never knew existed comes to him: a girl of 20. His youth is restored.

The discovery (through birth certificate needed for passport) that she is not his daughter (a year out on calculation).

Conclusion?

Possibly that through believing it she has become it.

Possibly also, his wife returns to him.

Possibly they marry.

Emphasis to go on the father-daughter relationship.

Possibly reduce it all in scale: he is the proprietor of a sporting goods store. Or the owner of an uninteresting business in Philadelphia or Boston.

Two people whom life has treated badly. Maybe she has been jilted by a married man. Companions in adversity. The perfect combination: mature wisdom with youthful freshness.

Love without the complications.

This note was undated, but it was undoubtedly not later than 1938. For one thing, Barry himself was forty-two in that year. He had endured the six most discouraging years of his career having written four plays (*The Joyous Season, Bright Star, Spring Dance, Here Come the Clowns*) and a novel (*War in Heaven*) into all of which he had poured his heart and soul and deepest faith, and all of them had failed. But more conclusive evidence of the date was the fact that the notes headed *Daughter* were written on the first two pages of a small pocket notebook, and on the fourth page was the beginning of an idea for another play:

The Family in the process of being studied for a piece in "Fortune."

Most Unfortunate.

From those fifteen words emerged one of the most triumphant of American comedies, *The Philadelphia Story*, which was writ-

ten in 1938 and produced the following year. There was, of
course, a very incidental father-daughter relationship in that
play. Some of the speeches of the Philadelphia Main Line father
—Seth Lord—could have been spoken by Josiah Bolton, such
as: "I suppose the best mainstay a man can have as he gets along
in years is a daughter—the right kind of daughter . . . one who
loves him blindly—as no good wife ever should, of course.—
One for whom he can do no wrong—"

Phil and Ellen Barry had two sons who are now very able
young men. Their only daughter died in infancy, and this was
a dreadful blow. I believe that in Phil's fanciful imagination
this daughter lived and grew and one may see his concept of her
in girls that he wrote, especially Tracy Lord and Miranda
Bolton. The deaths of others close to him contributed to the
history of *Second Threshold*. When Robert Benchley went to the
hospital with fatal illness in 1945, Barry was one of the most
faithful friends in attendance. Subsequently, he started putting
down notes for a play about a tragic character resembling
Benchley. In these notes appear such items as "father-daughter?"
—"the two 'accidents'?"—which show that the Benchley idea
(a very different story, which was never written) was somehow
interwoven with the theme of this his last play, a theme that
stayed in his mind throughout the writing of *The Philadelphia
Story, Without Love, Foolish Notion* and the adaptation of *My
Name is Aquilon*.

The volume of notes that Barry piled up on this play is
prodigious, and particularly impressive to me, since I rarely make
a note for anything that I write, except an occasional jotting on
the back of an envelope, which I almost invariably lose; I operate
on the convenient theory that if I think of an idea for a scene
or a line of dialogue, and then cannot remember it, it was probably no good to begin with—and that, admittedly, is a sloppy,
lazy way to work. Barry was not sloppy nor lazy. For one pos-
sessed of such elfin, elusive qualities, he was remarkably metic-

ulous and tidy. He covered masses of sheets of yellow paper with
notes penciled in his tiny, precise handwriting. For example, the
first time that the entrancing character, Thankful Mather, appears in the notes, he put down a number of words she would
use in her dialogue: "Natch. Latch on to. Gruesome. Rugged.
Genial. Riveting. Ghoulish. Gorgeous. Loopy. Murderous." (He
had evidently been listening attentively to the chatter of the
young things at Easthampton and Hobe Sound.) As it happened, not one of those words was in the play as he finally
wrote it.

The notes contain more than thirty different titles for *Second
Threshold*. The earliest of them was *The Salt and the Savor*. After
that the play was called *The Saving Grace* and then, *Stern
Daughter*. He always accompanied the title with the designation,
"A Comedy in Three Acts." In one of his earliest scenarios he
wrote that Josiah's arrival "at the end of his soul's rope" was due
to the fact that he had lost his sense of humor, and when this is
restored by his daughter, he is saved. Here we have a marvelous
demonstration of the ability of a character, created by an author,
to take the bit between his teeth and bolt from the author's pre-
conceived notions; for, as we meet Josiah in the first scene, we
observe that he appears to have lost everything that makes life
worth living *except* his sense of humor.

Although Phil Barry had talked to me a little about *Second
Threshold* in the last months of his life, I did not read it until
after his death. It moved me very powerfully and excited me
greatly. For I felt that he had at last begun to achieve the realiza-
tion, or the synthesis, of his apparently but not actually dis-
cordant qualities: his Irish, impish sense of comedy, and his pro-
found, and also Irish, sense of the ultimate sadness of life on
earth, the "endless assault" of evil upon good. I think that the
most obvious mark of his self-imposed limitations had been his
fear that he must keep these two senses in airtight compartments,
that he had said to himself, as he started a play, "Now I'll write

a comedy (or potboiler)," or "Now I'll write a serious play (or
valiant failure)"; and the comedies were far bigger than pot-
boilers, and the serious plays were far bigger than failures. In
Second Threshold, it seems to me, he began to reveal the mature
discovery that life is indivisible, that bright comedy and dark
tragedy must blend into the fluent half-tones which evolve between black and white and provide the endlessly varied colora-
tion of all creation. The revealing of this discovery in *Second
Threshold* makes his sudden death all the graver a loss to American letters.

The identification of Barry's protagonist, Josiah Bolton, as a
former high official in the Government inevitably stirs thoughts
of the tragedies of John G. Winant and James V. Forrestal (the
latter another close friend of Phil's). However, as we have seen,
the concept of the man "at the end of his soul's rope" had lived
in Barry's mind long before either of these tragedies, even before
there was a Second World War. Certainly the losing of the life-
impulse, permanently or temporarily, by a middle-aged man is
by no means limited to veterans of the interminable Battle of
Washington. It is known to many who have reached what is
mystifyingly known as "a certain age." Those who knew Phil
Barry best are agreed that he put a great deal of himself into this
complex character. He put in a great many other sensitive people
as well who will recognize something of themselves when they
see or read this play. Brooks Atkinson in *The New York Times*
described *Second Threshold* as "a genuine drama written out of
private brooding that gets down close to the fundamental
anguish of a thinking human being." John Mason Brown wrote,
in the *Saturday Review of Literature*, that in his concept of
Josiah Bolton's "death wish" Barry "had success no less than
power in mind and the artist as much as the government official."

It has been extremely interesting to me that while some have
found this play "obscure" or "perplexing"—Mr. Atkinson wrote
that "the clarifying word is never spoken"—I have talked to or

read no intelligent observer, Mr. Atkinson included, who failed to understand fully and to appreciate all of the major points and counterpoints. I venture to quote Mr. Atkinson at length:

"Second Threshold" comes closer than anything else Mr. Barry wrote to expressing the nebulous longing that permeated his whole career. Love is the genius of all human relationships. Mr. Barry was a moralist. He needed something warmer and more substantial than wit and cleverness to satisfy his troubled spirit. There was a moral tone to his most successful comedies of manners—"Paris Bound," "Holiday" and "The Philadelphia Story"—although theatregoers took away from them general impressions of gaiety and smartness.

Most playwrights would have been satisfied with the bright pleasure these comedies bestowed on the thousands of people who royally enjoyed them. But some deeper need drove Mr. Barry to write plays of religion and philosophy. "John," "White Wings," "Hotel Universe," "The Joyous Season" and "Here Come the Clowns" were the plays he put his heart into most sincerely. They were not only unsuccessful: they were not understood. By an irony of popular favor, Mr. Barry will continue to be known as the author of brilliant comedies of manners.

As far as that goes, "Second Threshold" looks and sounds like a comedy of manners. The characters are rich; they move in exalted social circles. They give and take property indifferently. The dialogue is written with humorous and elliptical grace. The characters seldom meet an issue frankly, but spin away from it in a flutter of mocking raillery. Since Mr. Barry was master of this medium and since he had both the taste and skill to write in a light style, the spirit of "Second Threshold" is beguiling. No matter what his private

mood may have been, Mr. Barry's code of manners en-
joined him from boring an audience. From a philo-
sophical point of view he was writing a problem play
in "Second Threshold," but instinctively he spared the
audience proof and argument.

The work of revision that I did on *Second Threshold* was in
the nature of carpentry rather than creation. Indeed, my ideas
for revision agreed with many that had been expressed by Phil
before his death; he always did a great deal of rewriting of his
plays when they "got on their feet," which means when they
arose from the typewritten pages into the mouths and minds of
actors, in the weeks of rehearsals and of tryouts before the
opening in New York.

What I have done on this play has been generously described
as "a labor of love." I venture to protest that, despite my affection for Phil and Ellen Barry, it was no such thing. I was im-
pelled solely by a sense of professional obligation. When I read
it I knew that it must have a hearing and, since I was asked to
undertake the job, I could not well refuse.

I was often urged to change the title, which was considered
puzzling, and the word "threshold" difficult to articulate. But I
couldn't bring myself to change it, for I firmly believed that it
was on a second threshold that Phil Barry was standing when he
died. I believe that had he lived to see this one through, he would
have gained a new confidence, a new understanding of the qualities that were his, a new ability to employ them to the full.

All of the American theater mourns his loss, and the absence
of all that he did not live to write.

ALFRED DE LIAGRE, JR.

presents

CLIVE BROOK

in

SECOND THRESHOLD

with

MARGARET PHILLIPS

and

HUGH REILLY

By PHILIP BARRY

With Revisions by ROBERT E. SHERWOOD

Staged by MR. DE LIAGRE
Scenery and Lighting by DONALD OENSLAGER
Production Associate, PHILIP BARRY, JR.

CAST
(In the Order of Their Appearance)

TOBY WELLS .... HUGH REILLY

MALLOY .... GORDON RICHARDS

MIRANDA BOLTON .... MARGARET PHILLIPS

JOSIAH BOLTON .... CLIVE BROOK

THANKFUL MATHER .... BETSY VON FURSTENBERG

JOCK BOLTON .... FREDERICK BRADLEE

First New York performance at the Morosco Theatre,
Tuesday Evening, January 2, 1951

Action and Scene

The action of the play takes place in the Library of Josiah Bolton's house on West Tenth Street, New York, in the course of twenty-four hours, late in July. The scenes are as follows:

ACT I

   Scene 1: Friday night.

   Scene 2: Saturday noon.

ACT II

   Scene 1: Saturday evening.

   Scene 2: Saturday night.

ACT I

SCENE 1

The Library of JOSIAH BOLTON's *house on West Tenth Street, New York, is a moderately large, well-proportioned room in the rear of the house, looking out over a small garden through tall window-doors giving onto an iron-work balcony, the room itself being on the second floor.*

The main entrance is through double doors from the hall in the center. There is a handsome old fireplace in the right wall. The left wall has two French windows. Bookshelves run from floor to ceiling but are broken by cabinets on either side of the center door.

The decoration and furnishings of the room are largely Victorian, but not entirely so, there being an occasional good English or French piece to save it from being too rigidly period. It is, on the whole, a comfortable, handsome, liveable room which has been put away for the summer, chairs and sofa slip-covered, chandelier and the two or three paintings are covered with tarletan. There is a tray with a thermos carafe of milk and a plate of sandwiches on a table behind the sofa. The time is late July, a Friday night, a little after midnight.

At Rise: TOBY WELLS *is seated in the center chair, listening intently, head cocked in the direction of the door. He is in his late twenties, spare, rangy, with a humorous, likeable face, not at all handsome. He is coatless, with necktie awry and shirt sleeves rolled up.*

3

> MALLOY, *a small, wiry, bright-eyed, white-haired man of sixty-five, comes along the hall from downstairs, a suitcase in each hand and a smaller one under one arm. He wears dark trousers and a black alpaca coat. As he sees* TOBY *in the room he enters.*

MALLOY

I thought surely you'd be left by this time.

TOBY

Oh, Malloy, is it Miss Bolton?

MALLOY

It is. She's stopped in the kitchen to speak to Mrs. Malloy.

TOBY

She's alone?

MALLOY

She is.

TOBY

You didn't say I was here—

MALLOY

Thinking you were not, I did not.

TOBY

Go on up. But quietly. He may be asleep.

MALLOY

> *Skeptical*

You think that, Doctor?

TOBY

> *Smiles, wearily*

No.

MALLOY
Too bad.

> MALLOY *goes out, upstairs.* TOBY *waits a moment, then crosses to the door and looks down toward the staircase. He then crosses to upper left window and looks out.*
> MIRANDA BOLTON *appears. She comes directly into the room, switching on the chandelier light.* TOBY *turns to meet her. She is surprised to find anyone in the room.*

MIRANDA
Oh! Good evening.
> *Pleasantly*

TOBY
Good evening.

MIRANDA
> *She comes closer to* TOBY, *smiles*
Why, I think I know you.

TOBY
There was a time—quite a few years ago.

MIRANDA
I've forgotten your name. Could you help me out on that?

TOBY
Gladly. I'm by name of Toby Wells.

MIRANDA
You're not Dr. Wells's little boy!
> *He smiles and nods, extends his hand. She shakes it.*
But of course. That summer at Christmas Cove. You had a crew cut—you were an absolute darling.

TOBY

That's right—I did have a crew cut.

MIRANDA

You used to bring me things: bunches of field flowers and pails of clams. I was so pleased . . .

TOBY

Don't mention it.

MIRANDA

I was flattered—because you were an older man, then.

TOBY

Sure. I was pushing twenty-one.

MIRANDA

And I was pushing sixteen.

TOBY

You were—advanced for your age—

MIRANDA

    Laughs

I'm afraid I've always been that.

    She sees the food.

Food, heaven!

    As she goes to it, she looks around.

Oh—how I love this house! All my life—the same home base. But it certainly could do with a little brightening right now.

    MIRANDA *pours herself some milk.*

TOBY

You haven't been here much recently . . .

MIRANDA

Not much. But I always love to come back to it. What have *you* been up to all these years?

TOBY
Johns Hopkins—University of Edinburgh—Navy.

MIRANDA
You're a doctor, too!

TOBY
Well, yes.

MIRANDA
Suddenly worried
Why are you here?

TOBY
My father's away on his vacation. I've been dropping in every now and then.

MIRANDA
Why—is anything the matter—?

TOBY
Just friendly visits. Your father tells me you're a Bachelor of Arts now. Congratulations.

MIRANDA
Thank you.

TOBY
Did you like Bennington?

MIRANDA
Very much. I had some experience with your trade. I spent my winter period in the psychiatric ward at Massachusetts General.

TOBY
Oh? I didn't know you were troubled that way.

MIRANDA
> *Laughs*
Working, stupid. And hard.

TOBY
I also gather that further congratulations may be in order.

MIRANDA
Thanks, they are. I'm sailing tomorrow night. We're being married soon after I land—July thirtieth. Isn't it nice?

TOBY
Just lovely. But I thought weddings usually took place *Chez* Bride.

MIRANDA
Oh, he's much too busy to get away.

MALLOY
> *From the hall*
Will that be all, Miss Miranda?
> *He stops in the doorway on his way down.*

MIRANDA
Oh, Malloy! Bless you. That food was a great idea. Thank Mrs. Malloy for me.

MALLOY
Will you be wanting her to wait up for your house guest?

MIRANDA
Oh, no—you neither. I gave her a key to the front door. Good night, you angel.

MALLOY
Good night, Miss Miranda.
> *He goes out.*

MIRANDA

I'm carting a girl to England with me—freshman at Bennington
—darling child: Thankful Mather. That's actually her name—
Thankful. Isn't that Boston for you?

TOBY

Do people still call you Mandy?

MIRANDA

No, they do not.

TOBY

Too bad. You were awfully nice when you were Mandy.
She is not quite sure what he meant by that one.

MIRANDA

I'm sorry, Dr. Wells—I'm sorry I've changed so much.

TOBY

I used to be known to you as Toby.

MIRANDA

Whatever you used to be—
*TOBY takes hold of her by the shoulders and turns her
around.*

TOBY

Would you mind—turning around?

MIRANDA

Smiling, puzzled
Not at all. Only—
TOBY lifts the back of her dress.
Aren't we being a trifle familiar?

TOBY

I just wanted to see if you still have freckles on your shoulder
blades.

MIRANDA

Of course. I'd forgotten. You're a doctor.
>   *She smiles and starts toward the door.*
It's been terribly nice seeing you again. Do drop in at any time.
And give my best remembrances to your father, won't you?

TOBY

Very brisk, aren't you? Where do you think you're going?
>   *She turns and looks at him. She is now moderately
>   annoyed.*

MIRANDA
Now?

TOBY
Now.

MIRANDA

To see my father before I fold for the night.

TOBY
Sit down.

MIRANDA
I beg your pardon?

TOBY
The hope is he's asleep.

MIRANDA
How do you mean the hope?

TOBY
He hasn't been getting much lately. Sit down please.

MIRANDA
Well. All right.
>   *She sits.*

TOBY
Why have you walked out on your father?

MIRANDA
> *Astounded*

Why have I walked out . . .

TOBY
You needn't repeat my question. All you have to do is answer it!

MIRANDA
> *Smiles*

When you were at Medical School, dear Doctor, did they include a course in charm?

TOBY
Yes. But I flunked it. Must I ask you again—?

MIRANDA
No. I did not walk out on my father. He deliberately cut himself off from me—from everybody. That was his own choice— and it's his lookout, isn't it?

TOBY
He's got no lookout left. That's the trouble.

MIRANDA
What's the matter with him?

TOBY
Your father's hit a blank spot—a very blank spot—where he pulls up short and says, "Well, here I am. But where the hell am I? Where do I go from here?"

MIRANDA
Or—what do I settle for, maybe?

TOBY

Maybe. And what he settles for is the conclusion that life just isn't worth living.

MIRANDA

I don't believe it.

TOBY

I'm sure it's difficult, for the highly intellectual daughter of an even more highly so father—

MIRANDA

You're trying to tell me that he's cracked up?

TOBY

Not precisely that—but something like it.

MIRANDA

I don't believe it. Not him. A man as big as that.

TOBY

It's the big ones—the ones who've been in the so-called high places—who get smacked the hardest. They know what combat really is. They've been in the ring with the champ.

MIRANDA

Has he been talking about my engagement?

TOBY

A little.

MIRANDA

What has he told you?

TOBY

Nothing definite. But I gather that he doesn't like the idea of your going to England to marry a man old enough to be your—

Her eyes flash at him.

—a man twice your age.

MIRANDA
I'm marrying Matthew with my eyes wide open. And his age is
my business—or isn't it?

TOBY
That's for you to say.

MIRANDA
You're damned right it is!
            She is now moving about, nervously.
My father used to be very fond of Matthew. He respected him.
They worked together during the war, and after it. It was only
when Father quit his job that they drifted apart.

TOBY
Would you mind telling me—remember, I'm only a doctor—
you know, completely clinical—

MIRANDA
You want another look at my freckles?

TOBY
Not this time. Something deeper . . .

MIRANDA
Come on—what is it?

TOBY
Your relationship with your father—

MIRANDA
            She knows in her heart what's coming.
What about it?

TOBY
You and he used to be very close to each other—
            MIRANDA *looks at him sharply.*

MIRANDA

Now, listen—dear Doctor—are you suggesting—?

TOBY

I'm doing the asking, please. You've worked in a psychiatric ward—you ought to know that the doctor does the asking.

MIRANDA

But not the guessing! If you're leaping to the obvious conclusion that there's ever been anything Freudian in this family—then you'd better go right back to Johns Hopkins and specialize in osteopathy. There was never anything like that. As a matter of fact, it was the exact opposite. We were friends—companions. Nothing emotional. We were close to each other because I was the only member of the family he could trust *not* to be emotional. After Mother got a divorce, and he lost all hope of making anything out of Jock—you remember my brother, Jock?

TOBY

Nods

Sure.

MIRANDA

Father had me with him in Washington—he took me along to the conferences. I was useful to him: I'll say that for myself—secretary, hostess, courier, sounding board—mostly sounding board. He could talk to me, impersonally, about anything. That's the way it always was between us—impersonal.

TOBY

That's the way it is now, apparently.

MIRANDA

Exactly!

TOBY

You didn't come home for Christmas, did you?

MIRANDA

How did you know I didn't? Has he complained about that?

TOBY

Oh, no. I happened to be here on Christmas. I noticed that you weren't.

MIRANDA

I went to England—a house party—friends of ours. Father knew I was going. He didn't mind in the least. That was when—when Matthew and I got engaged. To tell you the whole truth, dear Doctor, Father has made it increasingly clear that he wanted to be by himself. Even after the accident, he insisted I shouldn't come down from college.

TOBY

Which accident?

MIRANDA

Last March—when he crashed that little chartered plane. I know it wasn't serious, but—look! Do you suppose there might have been a concussion or something?

TOBY

Shaking his head

We went over him like a dog for ticks. Nothing but a sprained wrist, minor abrasions and contusions. It was miraculous. They say the airplane was a wreck.

MIRANDA

I never could figure out how it happened. He's a marvelous pilot.

TOBY

I suppose we all get careless.

MIRANDA
Not him!
>> She looks sharply at Toby.
Do you want me to believe that perhaps it wasn't an accident?

TOBY
>> Ignoring the question
When did you last hear from him?

MIRANDA
Oh—a month or so ago. What's he doing—all alone—here—in the middle of the summer?

TOBY
He's been doing nothing—but—sitting and thinking—and reading—and eating a little at odd times—and sleeping a little at odder—and occasionally listening to the news on the radio. He hasn't stirred out of this house and its two-by-four garden in eight weeks. It was May thirtieth—Decoration Day—when he drove himself down the Island to Amagansett—"just for a swim"—with you know what results.

MIRANDA
I'm afraid I don't.

TOBY
Ask him. Possibly he may not want people to—anyway, it also turned out not to be serious—

MIRANDA
Are you trying to scare me?

TOBY
Perhaps "arouse" is the better word.

MIRANDA
But what are *you* doing about it? Isn't it your job as a doctor to take care of him?

TOBY

It isn't my job. I don't come in here as a doctor—as a friend.
If your father thought I was here in my professional capacity,
he'd throw me out. Maybe *you* can persuade him to see a doctor;
I can't. And, by the way, I don't send in any bills for visits,
which is just as well, since I'm producing no results.

MIRANDA

What can *I* do?

TOBY

You're sailing tomorrow night?

MIRANDA

I—I might stay on a few days, and fly instead.

TOBY

It's a three-months' job, at the very least. Six months would be
nearer it. I suppose—there's no chance of postponing the wedding?

MIRANDA

It's got to be now, or maybe never. Matthew has to go out to
the Far East in August and there's no way of telling how long
he'll be gone or whether I'd be allowed to follow him out there.
       TOBY *gathers up his coat preparatory to leaving.*
You're not going?

TOBY

Afraid I must. Couple of calls before I go to bed.

MIRANDA

Do you think I could get Father to go to England with me?

TOBY

I doubt it.

MIRANDA

It would be wonderful for him—he has lots of friends there, people who know how much he really did in the war, and they're grateful to him. And if he and Matthew could only come face to face—

TOBY
> *Smiling*

It's a nice idea, Mandy. Go ahead—put it up to him. No harm in trying.

MIRANDA

You think I'm a stupid child, don't you!

TOBY

I happen to be very fond of children.
> *He goes to the door.*

MIRANDA

Dr. Wells—

TOBY

Yes?

MIRANDA

I don't believe a word of what you've been telling me—

TOBY

I'm sorry. You'll just have to find it out for yourself.

MIRANDA

But—
> *Emotional*

I feel lost—helpless. I don't know what to say to him. We're strangers to each other—my own father, and I. There's a great gulf of indifference between us. I don't know how to get across it. I can't even see what he looks like, on the other side.

TOBY

Maybe—when that gulf is increased by the width of the Atlantic Ocean—maybe you'll be able to dismiss the whole distasteful matter from your mind.

> *He opens the door, listens.*

I think I hear someone.

MIRANDA

Probably Thankful, in from her party.

TOBY

No, it's from upstairs.

MIRANDA

> *Scared*

Perhaps he's coming down.

TOBY

Well—good night.

MIRANDA

No! Please—please wait just one minute.

TOBY

Why?

MIRANDA

It's just—it's just that I don't want to be alone with him straight off. I've got to think.

TOBY

Ever try feeling, instead?

> TOBY *turns toward the door.*
>
> JOSIAH BOLTON *comes in from the hall.*

JOSIAH

Toby! You still here? Haven't you a home of your own?

> *He says this in the friendliest possible tone.*

TOBY
Now look, sir—you're supposed to have turned in.

> JOSIAH, *whatever the "certain age," is built like an athlete, one in good trim. He is a man who has borne many responsibilities, much success and many disappointments and seems to have been bent down by none of them, at least exteriorly. There is, however, an air of distance that suggests a deliberate self-removal from further future involvements, big or little. He wears a dressing gown over a white shirt, with no tie, and gray slacks. He moves directly to the desk.*

JOSIAH
I turned out again. Also, I seem to have run out of—

> *He takes a package of cigarettes from a box on the desk, opens it, carefully, glances up, sees* MIRANDA.

—Miranda!

MIRANDA
Hello, Father.

JOSIAH
When did you get here?

> *He crosses to her and kisses her lightly on the cheek.*

MIRANDA
About half an hour ago.

JOSIAH
How are you?

MIRANDA
Very well, Father. How are you?

JOSIAH
Never better. Cigarette?

MIRANDA
Thanks, I've given them up.

JOSIAH
Admirable.

MIRANDA
That depends on how you look at it.

JOSIAH
So much does.
> *He glances from her to* TOBY *and back.*
You two know each other?

MIRANDA
Of yore.

JOSIAH
Yes, of course.

MIRANDA
Christmas Cove.

JOSIAH
A good summer, that one.

MIRANDA
It was the last good one.

TOBY
Not a care in those days that a Bandaid wouldn't fix.

JOSIAH
They catch up with you, cares and so forth.

TOBY
Do they not.

JOSIAH
> *To* MIRANDA

Very pretty outfit you're wearing.

MIRANDA
Thanks.

JOSIAH
Very becoming.
> *To* TOBY

Don't you agree?

TOBY
Anything but a surgical gown, I'm a wild man.
> *He moves toward the hall.* JOSIAH *continues to regard*
> MIRANDA *coolly, impersonally.*

I'll drop by tomorrow, if I may.

JOSIAH
Of course. Lunch—dinner—anything.

TOBY
Thank you. Good night, Mandy.

MIRANDA
Good night.
> TOBY *has gone.*

JOSIAH
A nice boy.

MIRANDA
Would you say?

JOSIAH
I'm fond of his father.

MIRANDA

I once was of mine.

JOSIAH

Calmly

And recovered from it, fortunately. You're sailing tomorrow?

MIRANDA

Midnight. The *Queen Mary*.

JOSIAH

Good ship. I know the captain well. I'll call him. You and I usually flew, didn't we?

MIRANDA

We were always in a hurry.

JOSIAH

Aren't you now? Forgive me, I didn't mean anything by that. When is the ceremony to be?

MIRANDA

A week from Tuesday. . . . Father—

JOSIAH

Yes, daughter?

MIRANDA

Will you please go with me—or fly over, if you prefer—to be there for the wedding?

JOSIAH

Amiably

I think it's much better not.

MIRANDA

You're the one who's supposed to give the bride away.

JOSIAH

That quaint old custom is superfluous in this case. Matthew Atwater needs no donor. He just takes things. Where's he holding
the ceremony? Westminster Abbey?

MIRANDA

Some Registry Office, whatever that is. Sordid, probably. Father
—do you know that it would make me very happy to have you
at my wedding?

JOSIAH

It's very nice of you to say so, Miranda. But you're wrong. I'd
be a bit of a skeleton at the feast, and I couldn't pretend to be
otherwise.

MIRANDA

Toby told me it would be hopeless to ask you.

JOSIAH

That young fellow shows gleams of intelligence now and then.

MIRANDA

What was it you said to Matthew when he telephoned you?

JOSIAH

When was that?

MIRANDA

Last winter, when we got engaged.

JOSIAH

Oh, of course. Didn't he tell you?

MIRANDA

I gathered it wasn't very agreeable.

JOSIAH

He must have exaggerated. We exchanged the usual compliments
and courtesies. "So nice to hear your voice again." "So nice to

hear *yours.*" That sort of thing. No heads broken. He was most courtly in the manner in which he spoke for your hand in marriage. He gave me a brief summary of his financial position and prospects.

MIRANDA
But what did *you* say?

JOSIAH
I forget my exact words. As I remember, I congratulated him on being so well off in such times as these. However, I confessed to being familiar with the date of his birth. I felt obliged to tell him that I was not offering my daughter for adoption.

MIRANDA
You can be a real stinker, can't you!

JOSIAH
            Amused
It has been said of me. Matthew knows that. I'm sure he wasn't in the least surprised—or taken aback.

MIRANDA
You hate him, don't you?

JOSIAH
By no means. I admire him as a vigorous force in public life. He is intelligent, he is urbane, he is immensely successful—and he serves as fine a dinner as the present British law will allow. Finer in fact. But as a son-in-law—

MIRANDA
If you won't go to the wedding, I hope you'll give me just one thing . . .

JOSIAH
I want you to choose your own wedding present—anything—

MIRANDA

I'm not talking about that. I want the parental blessing on my marriage.

JOSIAH

Blessing! My God, Miranda, you certainly *are* getting old-fashioned.

MIRANDA

Marriage is an old-fashioned institution. I should treasure your blessing.

JOSIAH

It is not forthcoming. It is not vouchsafed.

MIRANDA

All right. I guess we've washed up that subject.

JOSIAH

Not quite. There's one question I've wanted very much to ask you. It's probably impertinent—

MIRANDA
Ask it, Father.

JOSIAH

Would you tell me—how much do you really care for Matthew?

MIRANDA

More than I can tell you. He fascinates me: his mind, his strength, his manner, his whole approach to life.

JOSIAH

That's a great deal to be fascinated by. But is it enough?

MIRANDA

For me it is. Why shouldn't it be enough?

JOSIAH

You're a rare girl, Miranda. For you it ought to be all rapture and magic and total beauty.

MIRANDA

I'm not the starry-eyed type; you should know that.

JOSIAH

No—I'm not sure I do. And if you're not, more's the pity.
> *He looks at her.*
Do you want me to speak honestly?

MIRANDA
> *Looks at him, quickly*
Please! Yes!

JOSIAH

I'm afraid for you, Miranda.

MIRANDA

Afraid—for *me*?

JOSIAH

You're by way of missing life altogether. The way I've missed mine, let's say.

MIRANDA

But you've had a wonderful one! Good heavens, when you stop to think—

JOSIAH

Not for my money, I haven't. With your penetrating brain, you should have been able to figure that out.

MIRANDA
> *After a moment*
You've always treated me as—as a mind, haven't you? Never just as a loving daughter.

JOSIAH

I don't wonder you object to that.

MIRANDA

But the point is, I don't. I think it's what has given me what-ever strength of character I have.

JOSIAH

Mentally, very advanced, I'll admit. Emotionally, still in the egg.

MIRANDA

The hell with emotion. It's sloppy and messy and to my mind it's completely—

JOSIAH

To your mind. What about to your heart?
        Again, her smile

MIRANDA

A stout, muscular organ, useful for pumping blood. What about yours?

JOSIAH

I'll grant you it seems not to lift as it once did.

MIRANDA

How long has it been since you've seen a doctor?

JOSIAH

Why—only a few minutes ago. You saw him, too.

MIRANDA

I mean, how long since you've had a real physical examination?

JOSIAH

Not long—let's see—it was last March, after that stupid crack-up. That really worried me. Miranda—you know that I'm a competent flier—

MIRANDA
Yes.

JOSIAH
Can you imagine how I could possibly have done a silly thing like that?

MIRANDA
We all can get careless. That's what Toby said.

JOSIAH
Oh, he referred to that episode, did he?

MIRANDA
He also said you're not eating nearly enough.

JOSIAH
Nonsense.

MIRANDA
You're thinner than you were, you know.

JOSIAH
I can only trust it's becoming.

MIRANDA
Did you eat any dinner, for instance?

JOSIAH
As it happens, I had a late tea.

MIRANDA
A late tea? How very British! Why you and Matthew ought to get on perfectly together.
>   *She puts the plate of sandwiches before him and pours*
>   *a glass of milk from the carafe.*
You never had a tea—early or late—except when you had to be polite in London or at Chequers. Here! I want you to sit down and eat and drink this right now.

JOSIAH
> *Amused*

What for?

MIRANDA

Sustenance—and because I say so.
> *A moment, when he takes a bite of a sandwich, washes
> it down with some milk, stares at the plate.*

JOSIAH

You know, daughter—this reminds me.

MIRANDA

Me, too. You used to take some looking after, in the past, and
not only in the food department.
> *He looks from the plate to her, then around him.*

JOSIAH

Other places, other hopes, other ends of days.

MIRANDA

We had great times together.

JOSIAH

We did that.
> *He leans over and pats* MIRANDA's *hand.*

MIRANDA

Do you ever hear from Mother?

JOSIAH

Oh—a telegram now and then. You know, she never had time
to write a letter. She's back in Santa Barbara. I gather she's very
happy. Evidently her new husband—the semi-retired polo player
—is good for her.

MIRANDA

And Jock—have you seen him lately?

JOSIAH

A few weeks ago, I think. I believe he's very busy.

MIRANDA

Did that hurt you much, Father?

JOSIAH

Did what hurt me?

MIRANDA

Jock—flunking out of law school.

JOSIAH

I made impossible demands on the poor kid. One of my many miscalculations. I wanted Jock to be a really great lawyer—an exponent of pure law, as opposed to a shrewd opportunist like me. But he wanted to get into something called "show business" —he preferred *Variety* to Blackstone as reading matter, and that's the way he went, and wisely, I've no doubt. Grease paint can be a more honorable disguise than the false faces that are worn by us lawyers.

MIRANDA

And what did you want for me? How have *I* disappointed you?

JOSIAH

I've told you what I wanted for you, Miranda. Love. The kind of wonderful, enveloping love that I'm certain you deserve. The kind that I never deserved—and never got.

> *He has been speaking calmly, analytically, objectively, as though he were talking about someone else. He stands up, looks at the clock.*

It's a little on the late side. You must be tired after your trip, and you probably have a thousand things to do tomorrow.

MIRANDA

Nothing in particular.

JOSIAH

One thing—you must go down to the bank and see old Clifford Evans. He has some papers for you to sign.

MIRANDA

What are they?

JOSIAH

I've made a formal settlement, as they call it, on you and Jock. It's no fortune, but the income ought to be enough to feed, clothe and shelter you—that is if your tastes aren't too—Oh well—talk to Clifford.

MIRANDA

I'm sure I'm very grateful. But—

JOSIAH

Also, I've got rid of the place in the country and have put this one on the market, feeling quite certain that all of us are pretty well through with them both, and prices are still up, and it seemed—

MIRANDA

Staring at him

"Putting his house in order?"

JOSIAH

Yes, in a way. Or—you might call it a gradual shedding of responsibilities—you know—with the purpose to regain the unbent shoulders, the elastic step.

MIRANDA

I'll take your gracious gift, Father, when I have that withheld blessing.

JOSIAH

The cash is already in the bank in your name, I'm afraid.

MIRANDA
It can sit there.

JOSIAH
As you like.

MIRANDA
Father—
        JOSIAH stops and turns.
It's quite possible that you didn't get out of that accident as
lightly as you thought.

JOSIAH
Accident? Oh—how can you get out more lightly than to have
a red-faced Bonacker lobsterman haul you out by the seat of
your swimming pants?
        She stares at him, puzzled.

MIRANDA
Lobsterman? Out of what?

JOSIAH
The water.

MIRANDA
Which water?

JOSIAH
Gardiner's Bay. It was still cold, and as a swimmer I hadn't the
staying powers I thought I had. It was just plain stupidity.

MIRANDA
Decoration Day, when you drove down to Amagansett—

JOSIAH
Yes. Then I did write you about it? I wasn't sure. No, child.
Physically, still intact. Mentally a bit confused, maybe—but

then—so is everybody else with awareness of how the world is wagging, and of his own incapability of making it wag otherwise.

MIRANDA

Do you remember that night in Washington when you wrote out your resignation to the President?

JOSIAH

I remember it well. Quite an eloquent document, if I may say so.

MIRANDA

I stormed and railed at you for being a quitter—but I certainly didn't know how completely you *had* quit. I didn't know that you were resigning from the obligation to live.

JOSIAH
            Looks at her steadily for a moment
Maybe it's a little like—I don't know—casting-off from all you've had and taking your bearings from new stars you can scarcely see. Does that sound too romantic?

MIRANDA

It sounds lonely. Lonely!

JOSIAH
            He crosses to the window.
Oh, I don't know. I expect there are compensations. Whistle in the dark enough, and sometime you may hear an answering one.
            He looks down into the garden as if listening.
Pleasant weather down there?
            No reply
Good.

MIRANDA
Who—Who's that?

JOSIAH

A vision—an apparition. Quite an intelligent one. It's usually around here. I talk to it often.

MIRANDA

Father—

JOSIAH

Yes, daughter?

MIRANDA

Father—why can't it be the same again?

JOSIAH

The same as what?

MIRANDA

As when—when we worked together—when we were close to each other—

JOSIAH

Harshly

Miranda! I would remind you of a passage from the Bible. It's one of the most beautiful, and also one of the bitterest—

MIRANDA

I never heard you quote a passage from the Bible in all my life!

JOSIAH

"If the salt has lost its savour wherewith shall it be salted? It is thenceforth good for nothing but to be cast out and to be trodden under foot of men." Think that one over, Miranda, and—go on your way. Pick up your things and move on.

MIRANDA

Then that's it.

JOSIAH

What's "it"?

MIRANDA

You think you're through.

JOSIAH

Me? Through? Josiah Bolton? At his age? Why, my dear, I feel as young as a pup and chipper as a cricket.

MIRANDA

You're lying in your teeth, Father.

JOSIAH

Some of which I still have—and don't you forget it!
The door opens and THANKFUL *comes in.*

THANKFUL

Oh!

JOSIAH *turns quickly to the door.*

JOSIAH

Well! What have we here?
A girl of nineteen has come quietly a little way from the hall. She wears an evening dress, and a light wrap, and is very pretty, with wide, unsmiling eyes and a single expression, one of somewhat puzzled intentness. This is THANKFUL MATHER, *in the delectable flesh. What goes on in her head, no one knows; what she has to say proceeds from elsewhere.*

MIRANDA

Still watching JOSIAH
Hello, Thankful. How was the party? As usual?

THANKFUL

Hi, Sweetie. I'm bushed. I'm absolutely beat.

MIRANDA

This is my father. Father—this is Thankful Mather. Needless to say—from Boston.

THANKFUL
Oh!

JOSIAH
How do you do, Miss Mather?

THANKFUL
I've always wanted to meet you, Mr. Bolton.

JOSIAH
I am most gratified.

MIRANDA
She's going with me on the *Mary*. I promised her mother I'd explain the difference between fore and aft.

THANKFUL
    To JOSIAH
What's it like to be parent to such a brain?

JOSIAH
Frightening.

THANKFUL
I'd perish—I'm really flattened, Miranda. I'm completely all wore out. Pity me. They dance so differently down here. 'Specially Princeton men.

JOSIAH
How in heaven's name old are you?

THANKFUL
I'll be twenty-one next month. No: I needn't lie about it: who am I fooling? I'll be twenty. Why?

JOSIAH
Just the difficulty of believing you're completely all wore out. It generally comes a little later.

JOSIAH *is* looking at THANKFUL *with amused interest.*
And, may I ask, why are you going to Europe? Are you getting
married, too?

THANKFUL
Married? Oh, dear no. At least, not as far as I know. I'm going
on account of culture.

JOSIAH
Good! Culture is much better than marriage. It lasts longer.

THANKFUL
Mother gave me a list of cathedrals and museums as long as—
as—well, you just ought to *see* it. But I'm taking my portable
Victrola and a whole stack of records and I expect I'll see *some*
American boys here or there—

JOSIAH
Undoubtedly—so the cathedrals and museums can wait—in fact,
they *will* wait, indefinitely.
            To MIRANDA
What did you say her name is?

MIRANDA
Thankful Mather.

JOSIAH
            Smiles
Ah, yes. In that case, good night to you both.

MIRANDA
Good night, Father.

JOSIAH
Good night, daughter.
            Kisses her
Sleep well.

MIRANDA
Also you.

JOSIAH
Why not? And you, sweet innocent!
                THANKFUL *starts slightly.*

THANKFUL
Me? Oh I always!
                JOSIAH *moves toward the hall.*

JOSIAH
May heaven's brightest angels watch over thee.

THANKFUL
Thee too.
                At the door he stops and turns to THANKFUL.

JOSIAH
Descended from the Reverend Cotton Mather, by any chance?

THANKFUL
Shouldn't be surprised.

JOSIAH
I think *he* would be.
                He goes out. THANKFUL *takes a deep breath.*

THANKFUL
Goodness, what an *attractive* man! And knows it, I expect. They
usually.

MIRANDA
No . . . no, I don't think he does at all. And that may be part
of it.

THANKFUL
Part of what?

MIRANDA

It's so awful. I've got to think it out. I must.

THANKFUL

What is? What must you? Do you like this cape? They come
in several weights, but I like this one. It's lighter than the
heavier ones.
>> *She lets the cape droop and passes a hand over her
>> eyes.*

Goodness! I'm still a soupçon dizzy.
>> *Takes off cape*

Principally I'm sleepy. If you don't mind I think I'll hit the
sack.—I'm sorry something's awful for you.

MIRANDA

I know you are, Thanks. But go on up to bed. Your room's one
flight up. Straight ahead. The little room on the right.

THANKFUL

Why, Miranda Bolton—look at you!

MIRANDA

What about me?

THANKFUL

Your eyes. Of course, I can't imagine *you* crying about anything. But—

MIRANDA

Cry! I haven't cried since I was five.

THANKFUL

I do when I feel like it. Sometimes they just, you know, bust
loose. I only meant your eyes look funny—starey, sort of.

MIRANDA

Go to bed, Thanks.

THANKFUL

I always let 'em rip. It feels good after, sometimes even during.
She half turns, then turns back again.
I only meant if there's anything I might do to help!—
There is a pause.

MIRANDA

What would you do if someone—if suddenly you discovered
that someone who—who was terribly dear to you, was in terrible
danger?

THANKFUL

Why, I—I think I'd try to *do* something about it right away.

MIRANDA

She turns away.
But if you felt so horribly helpless and alone!

THANKFUL

There's always *people*. That's the nice thing about people. So
at least I'd try to, you know, form a rescue party or something.
MIRANDA *looks back to her quickly. She explains.*
You know: like when you're skiing or something and someone
gets lost?

MIRANDA

Thank you, Thanks.
She sits at the desk and picks up the telephone.

THANKFUL

Suddenly
It's not—it's not *him*?!

MIRANDA

Him.

THANKFUL

You mean someone is—he's got an enemy or something?

MIRANDA
About the worst there is, I'd say.
> *To the telephone*
Southampton, Long Island, 4478.

THANKFUL
You mean a Public Enemy?

MIRANDA
> *To the telephone*
Algonquin 4-1098. That's right.

THANKFUL
Honestly, Miranda, I mean it: if I can help even in the littlest way—

MIRANDA
You're a good girl, Thanks. Hello—is Jock Bolton there . . .
Well, if he's asleep, wake him up . . . This is his sister, Miranda
Bolton . . . Tell him it's very important . . . Thank you . . .
> *She turns to* THANKFUL.
Please go to bed. Chances are I'll be up before you're asleep.

THANKFUL
I go right off to. But if you shake me a little—

MIRANDA
I promise to, if I need to. Good night, Thanks.

THANKFUL
'Night, Miranda.
> *She glances about her apprehensively and murmurs.*
Goodness!
> *As* THANKFUL *goes out,* MIRANDA *returns to the telephone.*

MIRANDA

Hello Jock . . . Yes . . . Look Jock, you've got to get up here tomorrow morning . . . I know . . . I know . . . But this is an absolute must. It's urgent. It's like a—an emergency . . . It's about Father . . . He's in bad shape . . . Oh, he looks all right —he's glibber than ever—too glib, in fact. But he's *changed*— you can't imagine how he's changed. It's—it's frightening. . . . Listen, Jock—I don't care if you do have a rehearsal, you've got to come. I promise you that if you don't, I'll hate you all my life . . . Hello! Are you still there? . . . Well, don't stop to think—of course you can . . . Ah, that's better—that's fine, fine! . . . Thank you, Jock. Good night, Jock.

> *She replaces the telephone. Her head goes down and her shoulders begin to shake and she sobs to herself.*

Oh, God, dear God—how I hate the ones who blubber!

CURTAIN

Scene 2

The Library, about half-past twelve the following noon, Saturday. The room is much brighter and pleasanter; both windows are open and the midday sun is strong outside. MALLOY *has removed the dust covers and tarletans, and is now folding up the last of them.*

JOCK *comes in. He is not more than twenty-three. He has a sensitive, humorous face, and his father's rangy frame. He wears flannels and a linen or alpaca jacket, none too neat.*

JOCK
Oh, Hiyah, Malloy.
He shakes MALLOY'S *hand.*

MALLOY
Why, Mr. Jock! How've you been? You're looking fine.

JOCK
That answers your question. Where's Miranda?

MALLOY
Upstairs. I'll tell her you're here.

JOCK
Thanks, Malloy.

MALLOY
You'll be staying for lunch?

JOCK
Sure—I guess so.

MALLOY
And dinner?

JOCK
Definitely not!

> MALLOY *takes the folded covers and goes out.* JOCK *walks around, inspecting the room with the air of one who has known it well but who hasn't been here in some time. When he gets to the windows and looks out, he stops short. He sees his father working in the garden. This sight amazes him. The voice of* THANK-FUL *is heard humming down the hall. She appears in the doorway and looks at* JOCK; *she is not at all surprised. She has her handbag over her arm, and is putting on white nylon gloves.*

THANKFUL
> *In door*

Hi—

JOCK
Oh—Hi—

THANKFUL
You're Jock?

JOCK
I have that distinction. And who are you?

THANKFUL
Thankful Mather. Bennington. Freshman. Well—now I'm a sophomore.

JOCK
Well done!
> *They shake hands.*

Friend of Mandy's?

THANKFUL
Yes—younger than, of course. But she treats me as if I were twenty-five—grown up. We're sharing a cabin on the *Queen Mary.* I've got to go shopping now. Kleenex. Do you know what somebody told me? They haven't got Kleenex over there! Can you imagine?

JOCK
I can't believe it! They *seemed* civilized . . .

THANKFUL
Have you ever been in Europe?

JOCK
Um-hm. Last summer. But I neglected to investigate the Kleenex situation. Sorry!

THANKFUL
> *Eyeing him, approvingly*

What do you *do* in particular?

JOCK
I'm an artist.
> THANKFUL's *eyebrows go up.*

I act. I'm currently appearing in summer stock, entertaining the yokelry of Southampton.

THANKFUL
That must be kind of fun—acting.

JOCK
> *He looks at her.*

Oh it's just like anything else. You know—work—boring. But

there's one thing about the theater—you learn how to handle
women. I might just decide to handle you.

THANKFUL
Laughs
Kind of crazy, aren't you?

JOCK
Kind of. And how about you?

THANKFUL
What about me?

JOCK
Are you crazy?

THANKFUL
I work at it, sometimes.

JOCK
Good!

THANKFUL
What did you see when you were in Europe? Cathedrals?
Museums?

JOCK
Oh, you can't miss those. I mean—they're there, right in your
way, wherever you look. But I saw eleven plays in London, and
six plays in Paris. Then I pushed on to Rome, but all the theaters
there had movies in them. Except the Circus Maximus, and they
told me that hasn't had an attraction since *Ben Hur*. So there
was nothing for me to see but sights.

THANKFUL
That must have been pretty frustrating for you.

JOCK
> *Laughs*

Don't let my hardships discourage you.

THANKFUL

I won't. But there's something I've got to know, Jock—is there a drug store around here?

JOCK

Sure—around the corner—on Sixth Avenue.

THANKFUL

How do I find Sixth Avenue?

JOCK

Well—you go out the front door—turn left—and start walking.

THANKFUL

Yes.
> THANKFUL, *with her left hand, rehearses her direction.*

JOCK

And if you come to a big, wide river, with ferry boats on it, you've overshot your mark.
> THANKFUL *laughs again.* She *is enjoying this conversation.* MIRANDA *comes in.*

JOCK

Hello, Mandy.

MIRANDA

How are you, Jock?
> *They exchange brief, brotherly-sisterly kisses.*

THANKFUL
> *To* MIRANDA

He's crazy! He's absolutely crackers! I'm wild about him. I've got to get some Kleenex.
> *She goes.* MIRANDA *closes the door behind her.*

JOCK
> *Laughs*

What was *that*?

MIRANDA

Just exactly what it seemed to be. . . . Have you seen Father?

JOCK

Yes—he's down there in the garden.
> *He takes a cigarette and lights it.*

MIRANDA

Does he know you're here?

JOCK

Don't think so. I just looked down and saw him puttering with flowers. That's a new one. He used to call everything petunias.

MIRANDA

You'll find some other changes in him if you look closely.

JOCK

This one I like. He's got a harmless occupation at last.

MIRANDA

Sit down, Jock.
> JOCK *takes his coat off, throws it on the desk, and sits down, slumped in the big chair.*

JOCK

You look to me, Mandy, like a girl with a very long story on the tip of her tongue. Kindly make it as short as possible. I've got to get back to Southampton this afternoon.

MIRANDA

You won't want to go back when you know how it is here.

JOCK

We'll argue that one later. Shoot!

MIRANDA

You'd better snap out of that beach-club lightheadedness, because we've run into something desperately serious, you and I.

JOCK

With a gesture toward the garden

He looks all right.

MIRANDA

Deliberately

However he looks, I don't think he has much longer to live.

JOCK

What's he got?

MIRANDA

Turns away, looks toward the garden

There isn't a name for it. You might say—spiritual malaise—in its most malignant form.

JOCK

Spiritual malaise my foot. You'd say something like that only if you'd been to Bennington.

MIRANDA

Trying hard to control her temper

There's every sign that he intends to kill himself.

JOCK *looks at her steadily to make sure she really meant that.*

JOCK

Coolly

I don't believe it. I simply don't believe it. Not him.

MIRANDA

That's just what *I* said to Toby, last night.

JOCK
Who's Toby?

MIRANDA
Doctor Wells's son. He's also a doctor.

JOCK
I remember him. He's not much older than us. He can't know
anything.

MIRANDA
He doesn't have to, in this case. He broke it to me as gently as
he could—too gently. Since then, I've realized it's much worse
than he said—much more immediate.

JOCK
What—did you find a gun in the desk drawer with one silver
bullet in it?

MIRANDA
For God's sake, Jock! You've got to see this plain—

JOCK
            Rises
And for God's sake, Mandy, why didn't you give me this baloney
on the telephone last night and save me the trouble of making
a long trip?
            MIRANDA *goes to the desk and picks up some legal*
            documents.

MIRANDA
Just take a look at this "baloney."
            She hands the papers to JOCK. *He glances at them*
            uncomprehendingly.

JOCK
What is it?

MIRANDA

Some legal papers. Clifford Evans sent them up from the bank this morning for you and me to sign. Father's signed them already.

JOCK

What does it all mean?

MIRANDA

Father has settled practically all his money on the two of us. It's all in cash. It's sitting there, in the bank, waiting for us to go and pick it up.

> JOCK *now takes his first real look at the paper and emits a long whistle.*

I'm not taking mine. Of course, you can do as you please with yours—spend it, give it away, hide it under a brick—

JOCK

This probably means nothing but some kind of a tax dodge. In which case, I'll be glad to co-operate to help the old man out.

MIRANDA

I was sure you'd be big about it.

JOCK

Is this all you have to go on?

MIRANDA

There's too much more, and it all adds up.

> *She turns to him with urgency.*

Jock—you love him, don't you.

> *That is not really a question.*

JOCK

> *Levelly*

No—I don't think I do. And why should I? Do you love somebody who's never given you anything but contempt?

MIRANDA

Plus a big allowance.

JOCK

Too big, if you ask me. It was conscience money.
          He brandishes one of the papers.
This is conscience money!
          He tosses the papers on the desk.
He had a God complex—thought he could create me in *his*
image. Well, it didn't work. I failed him, because I happened
to have a heart of my own and it just wasn't in the legal profession. Now, I guess, he's begun to suspect that maybe he isn't
God, after all, and he's trying to square accounts in the only
way he knows how to.

MIRANDA

I'd call you an ungrateful louse, Jock—if I didn't happen to
know you aren't a louse. You're just terribly wrong. Last night
he talked about you. He said he was the failure, not you—

JOCK
          Unimpressed
He said that, did he?

MIRANDA

And there was none of that God complex—creating you in his
image. He said you'd done the wise thing in choosing to live
your own life.

JOCK

Oh hell, Sis—I hate it—I hate not being fond of him the way
I used to be, when we were kids. He never had time to pay much
attention to us, and Mother was always all over us, but I never
had any respect for her and I had real respect for him. When
he did have time for us, he could do nice little human things,
like letting me hold the fish pole if there was only one, and the

day he bought some Indian arrowheads from an antique shop
and planted them in the garden for us to dig up and think we'd
discovered them, and he was sore as hell at Mother for telling
us the truth. If he'd only done one little human thing since I
grew up and disappointed him. Why—last winter I had a
terrific part with the Top Hat Players on West 79th Street. I
asked Father if he'd like to see it. He said he was sorry, he
couldn't get off any evening that week, when I knew he wasn't
doing a thing and he knew I knew it. He didn't even send me
a telegram saying kindest regards and best wishes.

MIRANDA
He's lost the knack for doing human things, including living.

JOCK
Turns to her
Have you figured out how he proposes to knock himself off?
*He is being deliberately hard-boiled to mask a sense
of growing alarm.*

MIRANDA
It will be an "accident"—

JOCK
Such as?

MIRANDA
Crashing an airplane on a bad landing—or swimming out beyond
his capacity to swim back.

JOCK
Oh—those accidents. You can't make a case out of those. Anyway, some people are what is called "accident prone."

MIRANDA
What do you know about that?

JOCK
> *Sits on stool*

It's a well-known scientific fact. Some people are just more likely to have accidents.

MIRANDA

Yes—jockeys or trapeze artists. Father never was one of those. He never was a gambler.

JOCK

He never was afraid to take risks. He wouldn't have got where he did—

MIRANDA

But they were always remarkably well-calculated risk. If he's "accident prone" now, it means only one thing: he's deliberately careless, reckless, he's gambling with his own life because it's a currency that has lost all value for him. "If the salt has lost its savour—"

JOCK

If he wanted to commit suicide, why wouldn't he do it simply? Why go to such elaborate lengths as chartering a plane to crash it?

MIRANDA

That's out of consideration for us—make it look like an accident —nothing messy. He would never do anything that was messy.

JOCK
> *Still scornful*

No. Always legally correct.

MIRANDA
> *Urgent, desperate*

Jock! Somebody's got to get through to him—stimulate him— revive him—make him feel he's needed.

JOCK
Who can do that?

MIRANDA
All of us. His family. Last night—after I talked to you—I called up Mother, in Santa Barbara.

JOCK
I'll bet she was a fat lot of help.

MIRANDA
She understood, all right. She said she always knew that if Josiah Bolton ever lost interest in his chosen mission of reforming the world—he'd be dead. She promised to call him up today.

JOCK
When she wakes up—which will be about 4:00 P.M. our time. Has any real doctor been called in on this?

MIRANDA
He wouldn't see one. It's got to be someone who loves him— whom he loves.

JOCK
Is there anyone left?

MIRANDA
Certainly no one, unless it's you and me.

JOCK
That narrows it down to you. Is he still sore about your marrying that Englishman?

MIRANDA
Not sore, exactly. I suppose—disgusted—

JOCK
Have you thought about calling the whole thing off . . .

MIRANDA

I've thought about it plenty—all night long, in fact. But it wouldn't do any good. I know it wouldn't. I couldn't fool Father. He'd think: "Now I've ruined her chance for happiness." And he'd be all the more determined to get himself out of my way. You know, Jock, I didn't think it was possible that I could be completely licked by anything.

JOCK

You're Father's own daughter, all right.

MIRANDA

I *won't* be licked!
> *She turns away.*
But—I wish to God Toby would get here.

JOCK

> *Following her*

Listen, Mandy. Why don't you face it?

MIRANDA

What am I trying to do but face it? And make you face it, too?

JOCK

You know I'm no good in this. I'm only the wayward son— the afterthought in his love-life with Mother.

MIRANDA

Jock! What a horrible thing to—

JOCK

All right—all right—it *is* horrible! But it's true! This is your problem, exclusively. I don't mean a thing to him—except as a kind of reminder of his own failure—and you know it. All he cares about in this world is you. It's like an obsession.

MIRANDA

That's wrong—it's fantastically wrong!

JOCK
Then why does he take on so about your getting married? Did it ever occur to you that maybe—

MIRANDA
Violently
Will you please shut up?

JOCK
Gladly.
TOBY *comes in. He immediately senses the tension.*

TOBY
I brought you a handsome wedding present, Mandy—a bucket of clams. Malloy's opening them.

MIRANDA
That's nice of you, Dr. Wells.
She crosses to the windows. TOBY *turns to* JOCK.

TOBY
Could this be Jock?

JOCK
Coolly
That's who it could easily be. You're the doctor?

TOBY
In a sense—

JOCK
Then why the hell don't you tell Mandy that she'll only break her own heart trying to haul Father out of the grave that he dug for himself.

TOBY
You wouldn't mind if he died?

JOCK
Emotional

Of course I'd mind if he died! He's my father. I wish to God
I *could* do something. But—Mandy—she's just kidding herself
when she imagines that any artificial, hypocritical displays of
affection will get anywhere with him . . .

MIRANDA

Be quiet! He's coming up.
          MIRANDA *goes to the window.*
Hello, Father. How's life in the open? How does your garden
grow?

JOSIAH
On the balcony, looking backward

Those steps are a bit rickety—but what isn't these days? Morning, Toby.

TOBY

Morning, sir.
          JOSIAH *comes into the room. He is in flannels and*
          shirt sleeves. He looks around the room.

JOSIAH

What happened to the dust covers?

MIRANDA

I asked Malloy to take them off. The house looked dreary.

JOSIAH

Good! Fine! He can put them back tomorrow—after you've
sailed.

MIRANDA

Look—we've got a guest.

JOSIAH
Turning

Why—Jock.

JOCK
Hello, Father.

JOSIAH
To what do we owe—and so forth?

MIRANDA
I asked Jock to lunch. Naturally—I wanted to see him before
I sailed.

JOSIAH
Of course—a final family party. Very touching. But you should
have warned me. I'd have broken out my morning coat and
striped pants.

JOCK
I must say you look wonderfully well, Father.

JOSIAH
And why not? I'm always well, barring accidents.
          A moment's pause. Then JOCK *ventures.*

JOCK
Look, Father—I didn't come here just to see Mandy.

JOSIAH
No?

JOCK
I—I've been anxious to see you.

JOSIAH
You don't tell me. What is it—a little matter of a little extra
money?

JOCK
No, for once. I—I've been kind of worried—

ACT ONE 61

JOSIAH

Good boy! There's nothing unusual in that, is there?

JOCK

I know. But this time—

JOSIAH

Go down to the bank and talk to old Clifford about it. Get some use out of your godfather. So few do.

JOCK

Only I thought maybe *you* could suggest—

JOSIAH

Not possibly. I'm not anxious to take on anyone else's troubles, being at last so blissfully free of my own.

JOCK

Mandy's told me what you've done for us, Father.
　　　Indicates paper
It's wonderfully generous of you—but that isn't what I wanted—

JOSIAH

You know, Jock, there's something I've learned in a long mis-spent life. It may be of some value to you, particularly in your chosen profession.—Never be enslaved by the factual—facts—statistics—they are chains. Once as a young man I made the trip down the Saguenay River in Canada. The guidebook said, "This voyage is made over seemingly bottomless waters, between the twin cliffs of Trinity and Eternity."

MIRANDA

Really? That's quite lovely—only—

JOSIAH

It added cynically and lamely, "Which rise on either side to a height of nearly two thousand feet." I can't tell you how that statement depressed me. Beauty once more destroyed by the factual. Majesty made piddling by definition. Life to the letter: brutal—intolerable—appalling—how do we endure it?

JOCK
Father?

JOSIAH
Yes?

JOCK
Why don't you get away from here—get out into the fresh air?

JOSIAH
Why not? As a matter of fact, I'm leaving here shortly. Figuring on a little trip.

MIRANDA
To England, by any chance?

JOSIAH
By no chance.—Arizona—to hunt. I'm waiting for a telegram from an old guide, name of Nelson—he knows every inch of those mountains.

MIRANDA
You're going out there, alone?

JOSIAH
With Nelson, I told you. He and I understand each other.
        THANKFUL *appears in the doorway.*

THANKFUL
        Calls down to MALLOY
Will you just put those in my room, Malloy?
        She enters.
Good morning, Mr. Bolton. Well—it was the darnedest thing. I got the Kleenex and tooth powder and—and things I needed

and it made a vast package and the man handed it to me and there I was, all bright-eyed and a bushy tail, when a boy came up to me—he had a corduroy coat on—and said, "Here—you're too little to hist all that," and he took it away from me.

JOSIAH
Took it away?

THANKFUL
Yes. And while we were walking around the block we got to talking and it seems he is an oil painter and I'd be very surprised if he's any good although he's kind of cunning. Well, when we got to the door here he said he'd like to paint *me*. Did you ever *hear* of such a thing?

JOSIAH
Never!

THANKFUL
I told him that was awfully sweet of him but I'm sorry I'm leaving for Europe. So then he said how about going to some Greenwich Village place around here for a drink and I said, "Heavens no, I can't stand cocktails before lunch, I mean they spoil the whole afternoon," and he said, "Me, too, I seldom drink in the middle of the hay."
        She laughs but nobody else does.
Don't you think that's funny?

JOSIAH
I don't think I quite get it.

THANKFUL
Well—he meant to say "the middle of the *day*," but—

JOSIAH
No—no, please—don't explain it.
        MALLOY *appears from the balcony.*

MALLOY

Lunch at any time now, Miss Miranda. Just a little buffet, on the garden terrace. Clams contributed by the doctor.

MIRANDA

Thank you, Malloy.

> MALLOY *goes down to the garden.*

JOSIAH

> *Going toward the door to the hall*

See you all later.

MIRANDA

Father! Aren't you having lunch with us?

JOSIAH

Thanks. I had some parsley in the garden.

> *He turns at the door, smiles amiably on all.*

You'll forgive me my unalloyed bastardy, all of you. But I seem to have forgotten my manners, dwelling so long among the savage tribes.

JOCK

What tribes would those be?

JOSIAH

Oh, you know, human beings generally.

> *He smiles at* THANKFUL.

Present company excepted.

> *He goes.*

THANKFUL

> *She looks from* MIRANDA *to* JOCK *and back to* MIRANDA.

Well! Did I say something wrong?

JOCK

No. But I did, to you, Mandy.

He goes up and closes the door.

You're right to be scared. That hunting trip—all by himself in those mountains—it's murder. I'm sorry I shot off my big mouth—

MIRANDA

Tenderly

That's all right, Jock. Take Thankful down to lunch.

JOCK

Sure.

Pause

Come on, kid.

He takes THANKFUL'S *arm.*

THANKFUL

I guess I'm out of step.

JOCK

Oh—you could never be.

THANKFUL

Oh, I'd love to do anything I could. I mean to be helpful.

JOCK

Fine, honey! Let's discuss it, shall we?

He pulls her out toward the terrace. MIRANDA *faces* TOBY, *somewhat defiantly.*

MIRANDA

I'm much clearer in my mind now . . .

TOBY

That's good. Last night, if I may say so, you—

MIRANDA
You needn't say it. I know what you thought. Now—I have some reason for hope.

TOBY
Where did you find it?

MIRANDA
This Arizona trip—had he talked to you about it?

TOBY
Not a word.

MIRANDA
It sort of brings things into focus.

TOBY
All too clearly.

MIRANDA
It makes me hopeful we can do something.

TOBY
We? Don't count on me. I had no training at Massachusetts General.

MIRANDA
Will you stop sneering for a moment and listen to me?

TOBY
Yes.

MIRANDA
You said this was a matter of three months—six months. We haven't that time. Father may leave tomorrow. And even if we had time, what could we do with it? Go on double-talking with him, always skirting the main subject but never touching it, and all the time he'd be way ahead of us. I'm going to find

a way to face it out with him now—today—honestly—openly. That's the only kind of treatment he'll ever respond to.

TOBY

Shock treatment?

MIRANDA

If you want to call it that. It's persuading him that he's wanted —that there's so much—there's everything—that matters to him.

TOBY

I don't think you'll find your father that easy to fool. You may end up convincing him that you're only trying to clear your own conscience—so that you can go on to England and get married—and leave him to live, or die.

MIRANDA

You're a peculiarly loathsome specimen, aren't you?

TOBY

Of course I am, and it's all due to education. I was taught that while a little learning is a dangerous thing, a little psychiatry is plain disaster.

He is close to her, speaking very earnestly.
You may have some reason for hope. It's any man's guess. But —don't count on any easy way out. There's no quick cure here. You don't know what you're contending with—

MIRANDA

I know my father better than anyone else on earth!

TOBY

You did, once. But he's got away from you, from all of us, from himself. It isn't any open and shut case of suicidal tendency. It's worse. It's a kind of death in life. And if you were the greatest living psychiatrist, Mandy—

MIRANDA
> *Flaming, spins around to him*

I told you nobody calls me that—

TOBY
Jock does.

MIRANDA
He's my brother.

TOBY
So he is.

MIRANDA
> *After a moment*

Haven't you an appointment some place?

TOBY
Yes—here—for lunch.

MIRANDA
You needn't stay.

TOBY
I needn't. But I will.
> *They are facing each other. She is flashing hatred at him. In one quick motion, he takes her face in his hands and kisses her. She stands off from him, eyes blazing.*

MIRANDA
If I'm not being too personal, just what the hell did *that* mean?

TOBY
Only my way of expressing furtive admiration.
> *He crosses toward the window.* MIRANDA *stands very still, her mind working fast in consideration of this odd development.*

MIRANDA

Thank you, Dr. Wells. It's a thought.
> *She turns to him.*

It's an idea.

TOBY

Come on—let's go down and swallow some clams.
> *She starts toward the window.*

CURTAIN

ACT II

SCENE 1

The scene is the same, a little before six the same afternoon. The summer light through the windows is still of a volume to keep the room bright.

JOSIAH, now wearing a light summer suit, is reading a two-page telegram. He smiles slightly, puts the telegram on the desk, goes to the window, looks down, listens.

JOSIAH

Of course I do. It's all very touching—all very transparent. And quite natural. They think it's suicide. That's an ugly word, isn't it? Whereas—if the old man were to die a nice, quiet, natural death—now, how do you suppose they'd feel about that, eh?—I agree. They would feel sorry—a little . . . Oh, you're going? . . . Well, so am I. But we'll meet again—
> *He waves pleasantly toward the garden. Then he crosses to the gun cabinet, looks inside as* MALLOY *comes in.*

MALLOY

You're wanted on the telephone, sir.

JOSIAH

> *Turning quickly*

Please. Please don't do it to me, Malloy.

MALLOY

But it's Washington—it's the Department again, sir. They seem most insistent.

JOSIAH

Are they still on?

MALLOY

They are.

JOSIAH

How did they get the new number? Is there no—

MALLOY

Ah, these Governments have ways and means—unscrupulous as always.

JOSIAH

Smiles

You've discovered that?

MALLOY

And besides—there was a call Miss Miranda put through earlier— to Washington.

JOSIAH

Smiles again, but less amused

You don't say so! Well!

To the telephone

Hello. Yes, that's right, speaking. Put me through.

Then to Malloy

Hang up in the pantry.—And nothing more, nothing—unless really urgent.

MALLOY

Starts up and turns back

If I could rightly judge what you would consider—

JOSIAH
Just say sorry, unavailable. Take messages, if any.

MALLOY
Very good, sir!
>He goes.

JOSIAH
>Returns to the telephone
Hello. How are you, old man? . . . Fine, thanks. Couldn't be
better. How's it with the world?
>There is a pause. JOSIAH holds the telephone a little
>away from his ear, smiles slightly. Then
Such language! But who shall blame you? . . . Oh, just taking it
easy . . . Excellent . . . Like a baby . . . You should try it sometime. You'd be surprised.
>Another silence, then dryly
Why? What's on your mind?
>A briefer silence, then
Oh, no, I couldn't even consider it. Honored and all that, but I
can't—not possibly . . . "Personal reasons"—doesn't that still
cover it? . . . But of course! Any time . . . No, I couldn't name
a definite time right now. Certain matters may be coming up . . .
No, I'm afraid Monday is out of the question. Tell you what—
as soon as I know, I'll send you a wire. Let's leave it at that, eh?
. . . Fine—good!—Thanks for calling. God bless you, if He's still
operating. Goodbye, old man.
>He replaces the telephone, looks at it, puzzled, for a
>moment, picks up a copy of The Economist, goes to
>the chair in the center, sits down and starts to read.
>THANKFUL appears in the hall outside. She looks in,
>sees he is alone, and makes up her mind to do some-
>thing about it. She tiptoes in and, from behind the
>chair, she puts her hands lightly over his eyes.

JOSIAH
Starts
What the . . .

THANKFUL
Guess who?—I mean whom.

JOSIAH
Good Lord, I thought this game had gone out with parchesi—
Her hands tighten over his eyes.

THANKFUL
You've *got* to guess!

JOSIAH
He grunts.
Sophie Tucker?

THANKFUL
Laughs
Nope.

JOSIAH
Louisa May Alcott.

THANKFUL
Wrong again.

JOSIAH
Princess Margaret, you get right back to the palace!
*She laughs, removes her hands and in a quick move-
ment swings around and sits on the arm of his chair.*

THANKFUL
Aren't you *funny.*

JOSIAH
You think?

THANKFUL
Well, I certainly do!

JOSIAH
Well, that's certainly fine.
> *She gazes at him intently, her face about a foot from his, to his growing discomfort.*

THANKFUL
You know something?

JOSIAH
Less every day. But what have you in mind?

THANKFUL
I just can't make you out.

JOSIAH
I can't tell you how sorry I am.

THANKFUL
You aren't either, you aren't sorry at all.

JOSIAH
No?

THANKFUL
No. You're just saying that.

JOSIAH
I'm afraid I'll have to admit it. My small talk has a way of becoming microscopically so. Where's Miranda? Where's Toby? Where's—?
> *He starts to try to get up, but* THANKFUL *holds him down.*

THANKFUL
And now you're trying to change the subject.

JOSIAH
I'm a trifle confused: just what *is* the subject?

THANKFUL
You! *You* are.

JOSIAH
We'll get nowhere on that one. It's a sleeveless errand.

THANKFUL
Sleeveless?

JOSIAH
You know—like a sweater.

THANKFUL
All right: I give up.

JOSIAH
That's a good girl.—And go sit over there, will you?
　　　Motions to sofa

THANKFUL
Why?
　　　　Wiggles closer

JOSIAH
It will be less—congested.

THANKFUL
In a minute.—You know something else?

JOSIAH
Offhand, no.

THANKFUL
You wouldn't.

JOSIAH

Then that's that. So if you'll be good enough to be young and spry and remove your charming person from—

THANKFUL

What you wouldn't know, is that you're most ter*rif*ically attractive.

JOSIAH

Thank you very much.

THANKFUL

Don't bother.

JOSIAH

Very well, I won't.—But will you kindly tell me—no, never mind.—Look: that sofa is yawning for you.

THANKFUL

Tell you *what*?

JOSIAH

After a moment's reflection

Just why and what *is* this apparently mad current rush of young girls toward—I shall put it mercifully—toward somewhat older men?

THANKFUL

You think there's one on—a rush, I mean?

JOSIAH

I've observed it in various quarters, even in my own family. Of course, I've also observed that the men are usually either well-off or well-known. Not that I qualify in any such—

THANKFUL

Well, don't you think either one's more attractive than having curly hair or a seven-handicap at golf?

JOSIAH

I am merely asking for information, merely seeking enlightenment.

She gets up, circles above chair.

THANKFUL

Don't you admit it's being a little more advanced on girls' parts than on men's, who just keep on always being attracted to pretty girls just because they're pretty?

JOSIAH

Yes—yes, if pressed, I'm bound to say I do.

THANKFUL

Anyhow, *I* don't *like* curly hair or golf either.

JOSIAH

Flash the news to the Associated Press.

THANKFUL

What does that mean?

JOSIAH

It's known as a quip. Forgive it.

THANKFUL

Moves to the chair

Anyhow, you do think I'm pretty,

Sits on left arm

don't you?

JOSIAH

Why yes. Extravagantly. Do you mind?

THANKFUL

Not a bit.—And therefore kind of—irresistible?

JOSIAH

That, my dear child, is none of your business.

THANKFUL
> *Rising*

Anyhow, I just want you to get it into your thick skull that the world's just full of girls like me and for all you know there might any number of them be ready to be just crazy about you—and it's fun—within
> *She giggles*

certain limits, of course—and so why don't you do something about it? That is, unless you're dead on your feet, which would be silly at your age, don't you think?
> JOSIAH *rises, steps to left of chair and gazes at her, appalled.*

JOSIAH
Will you kindly inform me, who or what on earth put you up to—?

THANKFUL
> *Steps close to him*

I made a simple suggestion.
> *She raises her face.*

JOSIAH
> *Pinned against chair*

I—if you don't mind, I—I'm afraid I'll
> *He puts his hands on her shoulders*

—I'll tell you what—some rainy Sunday?

THANKFUL
> *Steps back*

So long as you don't miss the bus entirely. I'm not necessarily referring to myself.

JOSIAH
I hope not.
> *He leans over, takes her face in his hands and kisses her on the top of her head.* MIRANDA *comes in.*

MIRANDA

Hey! I'm supposed to be chaperoning her.

JOSIAH

Turning away

Don't let her out of your sight!

THANKFUL

To Miranda

Well—I've got to take a bath.

To Josiah

I'm evidently revolting.

She moves toward the hall.

Don't forget that rainy Sunday.

She goes.

MIRANDA *laughs. She considers this development encouraging.*

MIRANDA

Keep your hands out of that cradle, Father. You might get bitten.

JOSIAH

You mean—keep my hands out of the gears of that bulldozer. But you could learn a few things from her, Miranda.

MIRANDA

Amused

Such as?

JOSIAH

You believe in using your head. She believes in using other weapons.

MIRANDA

To tell you the truth, I lost my head a little this afternoon.

JOSIAH

Indeed? Where have you been?

MIRANDA

I went out with Toby—we sat on the terrace of the Brevoort.
It was heavenly.
          JOSIAH *is looking at her, curiously.*
We've been drinking white wine and seltzer. "Gespritztes," they
call them.—I think he's quite a dear, don't you?

JOSIAH

It's a word I'm reluctant to apply to my own sex.

MIRANDA

Sex.
          She has murmured it dreamily.

JOSIAH

What about it?

MIRANDA

Oh—nothing—

JOSIAH

You have a peculiar look on your face.
          She sighs and looks away.

MIRANDA

It will wear off in time, I expect.
          She sits on the sofa.

JOSIAH

Time for what?

MIRANDA

Oh—my wedding.

JOSIAH

Miranda, I'd appreciate a little clarification.

MIRANDA

Don't tell me you're interested! The man without interest in practically anything—

JOSIAH

I am merely inquiring what kind of a bug has got into you—
        She shakes her head firmly.

MIRANDA

No bug, Father, nor germ nor virus. Purely psychological—and sound psychology at that.

JOSIAH

Wine and soda, plus the heat.

MIRANDA

I had two and didn't even finish the second. Toby had to go over to Bellevue. Making rounds, or something. But it was cool there at the Brevoort—oh, so deliciously cool! I'll have to admit I'm a little disturbed, though.

JOSIAH

Too bad. The disturbed wards are full-up these days. Ask that amorous young doctor.

MIRANDA

        Pleased. Leans toward him.
How did you know he could be amorous?

JOSIAH

I'm simply a trained observer with a very good memory—at least one that goes back as far as Christmas Cove.

MIRANDA
> *Settles back*

It's quite normal, I'm sure. It must be related to the essential Id
and its desire to preserve its sphere of activity.

JOSIAH
Indeed?

MIRANDA
Knowing that in a few days I'll be married-up for life, I—well,
don't stare at me! Isn't it just as natural for a girl to want one,
as for a man?

JOSIAH
Want one what?

MIRANDA
One last fling, I suppose you'd call it.

JOSIAH
Not much time for flings, is there? You're sailing—

MIRANDA
Oh—I could fly over, a few days from now—if it came to that.
> *There is a silence. Then* JOSIAH *speaks quietly.*

JOSIAH
I don't think I'd try any such, daughter. Not if I were you.

MIRANDA
Why not?

JOSIAH
Not on that young man.

MIRANDA
But where's the harm?

JOSIAH
Not if you want your hair left on your head, my dear.

MIRANDA
So you think I might be the one to suffer!

JOSIAH
If there's any suffering to be done, I should fondly hope so.

MIRANDA
That's nice of you.
                    JOSIAH *looks at her, shrewdly, smiles. He sits down.*

JOSIAH
All right, Miranda—if it's a fling you want, have it, by all means.

MIRANDA
You wouldn't object?

JOSIAH
                    Lightly
Why should I? You're your own master—or mistress. Of course, it would be highly immoral, not to say contemptible. But so is the world. No harm in bowing to the prevailing fashion. But—

MIRANDA
But—what?

JOSIAH
No! I withdraw the "but."

MIRANDA
You were going to say something.

JOSIAH
I thought better of it.

MIRANDA
Think better again—and come out with it—whatever it is!

JOSIAH

I was thinking of Matthew—my dear old friend. I was about to
say—he might object to this last fling.

MIRANDA

If he knew about it, which he won't.

JOSIAH

Oh—he'd know, all right, the moment he looked at you. But—
in thinking he'd object, I underrated him. He'd understand.
He's *approve*! The whole subject would amuse him, vastly.

> MIRANDA *is not enthusiastic about the turn the con-
> versation has taken.*

MIRANDA

Then you think it's all right—for me, and Toby?

JOSIAH

I've told you—I think it would be all right—for Toby.

MIRANDA

You've given me up, haven't you? As a bad job. It means nothing
to you—

JOSIAH

I've done no such thing, my dear.

MIRANDA

You've given us all up—Mother, Jock, me—

JOSIAH

Ridiculous!

MIRANDA

Because we've given *you* up. We've run out on you.

JOSIAH
> *Looking at her, levelly*

On the contrary—all of you appear to be running *in* on me—
> *He picks up the telegram on the desk.* MIRANDA *darts a questioning look at him.*

I've just had a telegram from your mother. Listen to this:
> *He reads*

"Joe dear—distressed to hear you are not well."
> *He looks at Miranda.*

Now—how do you suppose she happened to hear that? Has my case been written up in the *Journal of American Medicine*?
> *He resumes reading*

"You must break out from behind that brownstone front on Tenth Street."
> *Again he looks at Miranda.*

How like your sainted mother! She always hated this house.
> *He looks again at the telegram and reads*

"Why not jump on a plane and fly out to Santa Barbara to stay with us but indefinitely."
> *He looks up.*

Evidently a question mark at that point.
> *He resumes reading*

"Martin and I would so love"—*Martin* and I would so love—"to have you and you could live in solitary grandeur in the guest house and have all the golf, tennis, swimming you want or, if you prefer, *canasta* and any number of amusing people."
> *He looks again at Miranda and smiles.*

I haven't seen the latest census figures so I don't know precisely how many "amusing people" there are in Santa Barbara.
> *He again reads*

"Do come comma Joe dear stop Love as always—Susan."
> *He puts the telegram aside on desk.*

Your mother was always subject to impulses—but whatever could have inspired this one?

MIRANDA

She loved you. If you ask me—she still does.

JOSIAH

Your mother never loved anything but her own possessions. As long as I could be listed as one of them, I sufficed.

MIRANDA

That's a nasty, brutal thing to say—and the first time I ever heard you say one thing against her.

JOSIAH

The truth is nasty—brutal—unbearable. And I'm reading no moral lecture. Your mother's passion for possessions was realistic. In fact, it goes back to the Tenth Commandment—"Thou shalt not covet"—that means, don't love and want what you haven't got. Follow that rule, and you'll be much happier. Look at me— I have nothing, so I love nothing. I'm a free man. By the way, no sooner had I read that telegram than I had a telephone call —from Washington! Can you imagine such a coincidence?
He is looking at her, keenly.

MIRANDA

Easily. I read somewhere that they're calling you all the time— they want you back, don't they?

JOSIAH

Quite possibly. Maybe they'd also like to recall General William Tecumseh Sherman. But neither of us is available. Well—after the telephone, I'm trying to curl up with a good book, when in comes—guess who? Thankful! Delicious little Thankful. You heard enough of that, Miranda. Some rainy Sunday!
He winks and makes a clucking noise.
What an entrancing prospect. Too bad I'll be away for a while.
He turns on her suddenly.
And—what's more—Jock insisted on having a talk with me.

That was while you and Toby were guzzling—what was it—
gespritztes? What *is* all this—this sudden concern for my wel-
fare?

MIRANDA
It's long overdue. We've let you down, Father—your own
children—

JOSIAH
Well, why not, in heaven's name? Who do you think I am—
old Mr. Barrett of Wimpole Street—that I should keep my children in chains?

MIRANDA
Your children have certain obligations that might be considered
inescapable.

JOSIAH
Rot! Mid-Victorian rubbish! Your obligations are to yourself
—and your God, if any. And—don't forget—in choosing to
live your own lives—you and Jock—you have liberated *me*.
There are no further obligations on my side either.

MIRANDA
That's precisely where you're wrong, Father. You also have
obligations to yourself—and you can't escape them by—

JOSIAH
By? By what?

MIRANDA
By—dying!

JOSIAH
Dying? Who's dying?

MIRANDA
You are.

JOSIAH

Thanks for the warning.

MIRANDA

Don't try to dodge your way out of this. We've got to look at things plainly, you and I.

JOSIAH

And I want to tell you, Miranda—that I'm sick and tired of all the moral regeneration that's going on around here. Even Jock! Jock—of all people. He had a burning problem. He amazed me. Said he had been thinking things over and wondered if he shouldn't give up the stage and go back to law school. Did you ever hear of such nonsense?

MIRANDA

I hope you encouraged him—

JOSIAH

Oh-ho! I made short work of *that* ridiculous idea. I told him—you could find no higher mission in life than to be an entertainer—singer, dancer—bring joy and gladness into this woebegotten world—have your name in electric lights. I gave him some good advice—stop chain-smoking and throwing drinks into you or you'll ruin your voice and cut your wind. Then I sent him packing off back to Southampton. "Never be late for rehearsal," I told him. You see, I know something about the theater. I once wrote the book of a Hasty Pudding Show and I starred in it. I had a number that knocked 'em dead.

   He clears his throat.

" 'Though I'm rarely in the money,
 It is really rather funny
How I always seem to land upon my feet . . ."

   He is doing a dance to this as TOBY *comes in.* JOSIAH
   says, "Sit down, Toby," *then continues:*

"When out strolling with my honey

On a day that's bright and sunny,
I invariably tell her she's a treat!"
>*He winds up with a slap on each buttock.*

Wump! Wump!

>*TOBY looks startled. MIRANDA looks scared. TOBY has not accepted the invitation to sit down. JOSIAH wipes his brow—then, to Miranda*

Funny?

MIRANDA

>*Solemnly, as she sits in chair*

Father, it's a riot.

JOSIAH

I was better with a straw hat—a boater—exceptionally broad brim.

TOBY

I didn't mean to burst in, sir! I—

JOSIAH

Don't be silly, my boy. Sit down. Join the party. We're having a fine time, aren't we, Miranda?

MIRANDA

Are we?

JOSIAH

I've been telling about the most thrilling day of my summer vacation. And I've just got something else—

>*MIRANDA looks at TOBY with an expression of desperate appeal, but he is watching JOSIAH closely.*

A telegram from old Nelson, the guide. We're all set. So—after I get you on that ship tonight, I'll be off to Arizona in the morning.

>*Crosses to the cabinet at the right*

You remember that big rifle I bought—the thirty-thirty—when I was going to Kodiak? That was a long time ago.

He has taken out the rifle.

MIRANDA
Father!

She jumps up.

JOSIAH
Before I could get started on that trip, some other people started shooting in Europe—so I never got to use this gun. But I clean it every day. It ought to be perfect for mountain lions. I believe there are still one or two left.

He sights the gun.

MIRANDA
Will you put that gun away!

JOSIAH
It's not loaded, I assure you.

MIRANDA
Put it away!

JOSIAH
Why, I'm surprised at you, Miranda. You ought to know I'm an old hand with firearms. You used to load for me in the duck-blinds on the Cape. What's the matter with you—gone all jittery in your old age?

MIRANDA
Have you made sure that this isn't the closed season on mountain lions?

JOSIAH
Oh—they're open the year round—if you can find them, and Nelson is the old bloodhound who can do that. But you have to go way up into the mountains.

MIRANDA
And if you never find one?

JOSIAH
    Excited
That makes no difference! It's the looking for it that counts. That's the real sport! All my life I've been looking—seeking— as who hasn't? And I don't look for the silver lining. The hell with that. For one thing it's inaccessible. For another thing— it isn't even silver. Merely a vaporous reflection. No, my young friends—what I look for is the hidden motive. The hidden motive in you, and you, and in me—and in life and death. Sometimes I find it. Sometimes the motive thinks it's hidden when it isn't. Then I can stalk it—silently, stealthily—till I'm within easy range—and then—
    He raises the rifle, slowly, sights it, squeezes the trigger.
BANG!
    He simulates the recoil of the powerful gun.
And another motive bites the dust. Look at it—lying there— quivering, twitching, still warm. Poor little thing. Once so young, so pure, so full of hope—and now—forever dead. Oh, God forgive me! Why did I do it? Why did I commit this murder most foul?

MIRANDA
    Violently
Will you put that gun away?

JOSIAH
Why, of course, if you *must* be squeamish. But let that be a lesson to you, Miranda. Sometimes it's better to leave the poor little motive alone. Live and let live—um-huh—or, even, live and let die.

TOBY
Could the medical department be heard from?

JOSIAH
Certainly.
He goes to the gun cabinet and starts to put it away.

TOBY
I wouldn't plan to leave tomorrow if I were you.

JOSIAH
Why not?

TOBY
My father's getting back tonight. I'd rather you wait to see him. Let him take the responsibility of authorizing a trip as rugged as this.

JOSIAH
Don't worry, my boy. I absolve him of responsibility. I absolve you. I absolve your whole family.

TOBY
You're a sick man, sir. You can't do it.

JOSIAH
Just watch me.
He has put the gun away and crosses to the desk.

MIRANDA
Distracted, to TOBY
Why don't you say it?
TOBY *looks at her, curiously. So does* JOSIAH.

MIRANDA
Go ahead and say, "I told you so." A little psychiatry—is disaster. Go ahead and tell me what a stupid, wretched fool I am—what an imbecile!

JOSIAH
But, Miranda—

MIRANDA
> *To* JOSIAH

I thought I could do something for you. Shock therapy! So I'm the one who gets the shock.

JOSIAH

But you have done something for me. Can't you see the magical change you've wrought? I feel marvelous! I never felt better in my life. And I owe it all to you. What you've done for me! You've shaken me out of this—you've put the old spirit of adventure back into me. And just for that—I'm going to take everybody out to dinner. Some place where there's music—dancing—*Noise!*
> *He goes to the door, looks up toward the staircase.*

Ah—look what I found in the hall. Come here, Thankful.

THANKFUL
> *From off*

I just had a bath.
> THANKFUL *appears, close to* JOSIAH. *He puts an arm around her.*

JOSIAH

She just had a bath,
> JOSIAH *sniffs*

she smells wonderful. Like a garden early in the morning of a hot summer's day. Thankful—Thankful—we're going out on the town. You and I are going to dance!

THANKFUL
> *Thrilled*

Dance? *Us?*

JOSIAH
> *Stepping away, hurt*

Miss Mather—I did not come here to be insulted. So you think I can't! Look!

*He holds up an imaginary hat, as if it were that old
Hasty Pudding boater.*

"When out strolling with my honey
On a day that's bright and sunny,
I invariably tell her she's a treat."

MIRANDA *has burst into tears.* JOSIAH *stops short, looks
at her.*

MIRANDA
Father! *Don't!*

As she runs out
I'm sorry!

JOSIAH
Miranda!

He goes up quickly.

TOBY
Mandy!

He starts as if to follow her, but JOSIAH *restrains him.*

JOSIAH
No!

He speaks quietly, with deep emotion.
Leave her alone. Leave her alone.

He looks off, upward, after MIRANDA.

CURTAIN

SCENE 2

The Library, about ten-thirty the same night. The room is dimly lighted by the one small lamp on the desk. The curtains at the windows are pulled. Here and there about the room there are pots of white geraniums, in full bloom. More light comes from the hall.

MIRANDA *is curled up on the couch, asleep.*

Voices are heard from below.

TOBY
Hello, Malloy. Is Miss Bolton upstairs?

MALLOY
Yes, I think she's in the library.

TOBY
Thank you!
          Calling from off
Mandy.
          He comes in, MIRANDA *starts up.*
Oh—I'm terribly sorry. You were asleep.

MIRANDA
I guess so.
          Yawns
What time is it?
          Looks at mantel clock

98

TOBY
Ten-thirty.

MIRANDA
That late! Is everybody here?

TOBY
No.

MIRANDA
Where are they? Gone to the boat?

TOBY
Evidently not. Suitcases are downstairs. I left the party an hour ago. Had some calls to make.

MIRANDA
How was the party?

TOBY
Terrific. I missed you.

MIRANDA
            Flatly
I'm glad you did.

TOBY
I wish you could have seen your father and Thankful. He was acting like a buyer from Council Bluffs.

MIRANDA
Is that a good sign?

TOBY
My guess is no.

MIRANDA
How did Thankful take it?

TOBY

Like a little man. Are you all right, Mandy?
She seems listless, depleted.

MIRANDA

Of course. A few internal injuries, perhaps. I put in a call to London. I was waiting for it when I suppose I drowsed off. Reaction to shock. Blankness. Why did you ask?

TOBY

I'd be delighted to take your pulse.

MIRANDA

I called Matthew. I'm going to tell him I'm not sailing tonight.

TOBY

         Amazed

So?

MIRANDA

I've found out I can get a plane reservation next Friday.

TOBY

Well, that's quite a decision. Have you notified the Cunard Line?

MIRANDA

Too late. Thanks can have the cabin to herself. My trunks are on board—but let 'em go. Matthew can arrange about them. He can arrange anything. I'll get there in plenty of time for the wedding.

TOBY

And in the meantime—what?

MIRANDA

I don't know. I'm scared.

TOBY

Maybe we could talk him into letting me go to Arizona with
him.

MIRANDA

Could you do it? Could you get away?

TOBY

Sure. I'm at loose ends after tomorrow. This is my vacation. I
could tell that guide a few things. Between the two of us, we
could keep an eye on—

MIRANDA

Looking at him, hard
And you *would* do that?

TOBY

I'd do anything for him. But—it's an empty gesture. He'd never
agree to it.

MIRANDA

There *are* some good people left, after all.

TOBY

Oh, sure. You run into them here and there.

MIRANDA

Toby—

TOBY

Yes?

MIRANDA

How about coming over and sitting here?
She pats the couch beside her.

TOBY

How about it!
He goes over and sits, as directed.

MIRANDA

I don't believe you're any great shakes as a doctor, Toby. But you can be powerful comforting. And—oh, how I need comforting.

Suddenly she puts her head against his chest.

Let me do this for a moment, will you?

TOBY

Go right ahead.

MIRANDA

You know—just friendly-wise.

TOBY

Friendly, certainly. But as to wise—

MIRANDA

Don't get any false ideas. You won't, will you?

TOBY

Hell, no. Not me.

MIRANDA

Understand—if you were just a post, I'd cling to you.

TOBY

Puts arm around her

O.K., I'm a post—hitch thou onto me.

MIRANDA

I've balled everything up so terribly. I feel so awful.

TOBY

You're wrong. You feel good.

MIRANDA

Don't joke.

TOBY

It's no joke.

MIRANDA

I'm so tired. Toby, I don't like myself any more.

TOBY

> *Amused*

Now, just a moment—

MIRANDA

No, I don't. I wish I was dead. I'm tired—if I could only have forty winks before we see Thankful off.

TOBY

Why not? She's hungry, she eats. You're sleepy, you sleep. Take Toby's hand—

> *He takes her hand, leans back into a corner of the sofa and draws her head down upon his shoulder.*

Feet up. Swing 'em around!

> MIRANDA's *head works more comfortably into his shoulder.*

That's it. That's the stuff.

> *Her voice becomes drowsier.*

MIRANDA

You *are* a good friend, Toby. Always be my friend, please.

TOBY

Sure thing. Now do as the nice, incompetent doctor says. Take deep breaths. Close the eyes.

MIRANDA

If life just wouldn't be so complicated.—It didn't used to be.—Remember the autumn day we went—cranberrying at Christmas Cove?

TOBY

I remember. Go back to sleep.

MIRANDA

And I—got stuck in the bog—and you were right there—with both arms to hoist me out?

TOBY

And one of my mitts slipped a bit. I remember.

MIRANDA

You were pretty fresh even in those days.

TOBY

Hell, woman, in those days I *was* fresh! Now, most likely, I'd just let you sink.

MIRANDA

Sink, sank, sunk.—I'm sunk now, Toby, I'm so sunk.—You would not. You'd do no such thing. You'd help me. You'd always help me.

TOBY

Might.

MIRANDA

Toby—why do you suppose Matthew wants to marry me? Why should he want to marry any such—ignoramus—me—

TOBY

We can never understand the older generation.

MIRANDA

That's an illegitimate crack and you know it.

TOBY

Indeed I do.

MIRANDA
I'm going to marry him if it's the last thing I do on earth.
She lifts a limp hand.
See my beautiful ring.

TOBY
Window-glass.

MIRANDA
It was his great-grandmother's.

TOBY
She went around breaking windows at her age?

MIRANDA
I'm going to be
Yawn
—good wife to Matthew—

TOBY
Go right ahead.—Only, when it comes second-husband time,
give a thought to home-folks, Mandy.

MIRANDA
Another yawn.
Don't be silly. You're being silly. There'll never be—second time
—Mandy Bolton.—But you're nice. I like you. I do like you.
I like you better than me.
And settles her head still deeper into his shoulder.
Tell me a story, Toby—

TOBY
What about?

MIRANDA
Now a small girl, half asleep, fading fast
Anything—just a story. You're an animal—tell me—an animal
story—
A moment. Then TOBY *begins*

TOBY
Remember how I told you that, after that first accident, we
went over your father like a dog for ticks?

MIRANDA
I remember—

TOBY
Well, here's a case history—a young woman was admitted for
observation. Rapid pulse, temperature one-o-one and two-fifths,
respiration normal, but with a most beautiful and extensive
rash. Measles and scarlet fever ruled out: both present in child-
hood. Upon routine questioning, was determined to be from the
south shore of Long Island and the possessor of two small, long-
haired dogs, pets, of the Skye-terrier breed. These animals she
cared for herself, exercising great pains to remove ticks twice
daily, it being full tick-season in that area. She had not worn
gloves nor employed any mechanical aids. It was a clear and
truly magnificent case of Rocky Mountain Spotted Fever, for-
merly, in humans, very often fatal. But happily we now—and
really just now—possess an antibiotic of remarkable efficacy
called aureomycine. And in a comparatively short time the
woman will be discharged completely cured and, we hope, somewhat wiser about the always dangerous occupation of removing
ticks barehanded. Wonderful stuff, these new drugs. But in many
cases, if I had to choose between them and the will to live, I'd
take the old original. And what do you think of that, for instance?
    There is no answer.
I say, what do you think of—?
    And still no answer. He looks down at her.
You mean you don't think a thing?
    She is silent, sleeping peacefully. He grins, speaks
    softly.
That's fine. All the same, it's nice we have both. All the same,

that rash wasn't pretty.—You're so pretty. Darling, if you ever have pups, promise me you'll be awfully careful with them, won't you?

> THANKFUL *comes in, naturally startled by what she sees on the couch.*

THANKFUL
Well, for *heaven's* sake—

TOBY
Sh!

> But MIRANDA *has started up.*

MIRANDA
> *She sits up.*

Oh, hello, Thanks. It's about time.

> *She crosses back up and switches on the light.*

THANKFUL
I should say it is. My, *my!* Toby! So that's the appointment you had to leave us for.

MIRANDA
Where's Father?

THANKFUL
He's in the pantry, getting some champagne and some food for me. I'm hungry.

MIRANDA
Didn't you just have dinner?

THANKFUL
Not a bite. Too exciting. Dancing. He's divine! My tum's right flat against my back.

> MALLOY *appears in the hall door.*

MALLOY
Your London call, Miss Miranda.

MIRANDA
>*Jumping up*

Oh—

TOBY
Come on, Thanks. We'll get out.

MIRANDA
No—I'll take it downstairs.
>*She is already out.* MALLOY *goes after her.*

THANKFUL
London?

TOBY
She's breaking the news to the venerable boy friend that she
isn't sailing tonight.

THANKFUL
Not sailing! Then I have to—you mean—alone—?

TOBY
You can take care of yourself, can't you?

THANKFUL
Well—I suppose—I could try.

TOBY
That's my brave girl. You know how to say "No"?

THANKFUL
No.

TOBY
That's right! Nothing to worry about. Miranda will be there
almost as soon as you—flying.

THANKFUL
Do you think she loves him—this Englishman?

TOBY

Well—when a girl as attractive as that marries a man twice her age she must love one of two things—him—or mink coats. Miranda can take care of the mink department on her own. So—I guess she loves him.

THANKFUL

And I'll tell you what *I* think, Toby—

TOBY

By all means.

THANKFUL

I think she's got a thing for you.

TOBY

Oh, you do, eh! What do you major in?

THANKFUL

Child psychology.

TOBY

I'll bet you end up giving lessons to the professor.

THANKFUL

Laughing in her own way
You're funny.

TOBY

Well! Glad I'm something.

THANKFUL

Well as long as Miranda doesn't want you—
She is coming close to him.

TOBY

Now, listen, repulsive—
Suddenly she ducks her head and lets her hair fall over her face, practically into his.

THANKFUL

Want to feel some silk?

> TOBY *passes a hand over her head.*

TOBY

Lovely stuff. I'll take the whole bolt.

> JOSIAH *comes in with a tray on which is a champagne bottle, some glasses and a plate of sandwiches covered with a wet napkin.* JOSIAH *barely glances at* THANKFUL *and* TOBY.

JOSIAH

Isn't it always the way. You fall madly, wildly in love with an entrancing creature. She gives you some reason to believe that your passion is not entirely unreciprocated. And then—the moment you let her out of your sight—off she goes with a younger man.

> THANKFUL *laughs*

You wanted milk, didn't you, darling?

THANKFUL

Oh, yes. Champagne's nice—but not when you're starving. It doesn't stick.

JOSIAH

Drink, Toby?

TOBY

Thanks.

> *He helps himself to a glass of champagne, as* JOSIAH *leads* THANKFUL *to the sofa.*

JOSIAH

A cushion for your little bottom.

> *He pats the sofa cushion. She sits.*

Here are sandwiches.

THANKFUL
Oh, yum!
>> *She takes one.*

JOSIAH
Take the whole plate. Eat your lovely head off.

THANKFUL
I often wish I could.
>> JOSIAH *watches her with pleasure as she eats and drinks.*

JOSIAH
Do you know what I feel like?

THANKFUL
>> *Her mouth full*
Am I supposed to guess?

JOSIAH
Not with your lovely mouth full. I feel like your beau at the commencement day spread. I'm bringing you chicken salad and strawberries and iced tea. We have just heard the commencement-day address by an important alumnus. He is a successful bookmaker, who has just been made honorary doctor of laws because he donated a million dollars to the college endowment fund. He has told the graduating class, "My young friends— you are standing on the threshold of life." How true that is! And then the years go by—"The years like great, black oxen tread the world—and God, the herdsman, goads them on behind" —and we come to another commencement and a grim orator saying, "My aged friends—you are standing on the second threshold—a doorstep into the final anteroom that separates life from death. Maybe it is an enormous room, the end of which cannot be seen, maybe it is a stuffy little alcove." So, let us reject this horrid thought.

He indicates a special sandwich to the munching, wondering THANKFUL.

Try one of these, Thankful—potted shrimps. Are you comfortable, pretty one?

THANKFUL
Oh—yes—ever so.
          MIRANDA *returns.*

MIRANDA
That overseas operator cut me off in the middle of a sentence.

JOSIAH
Miranda—when you were on the telephone just now—I want you to understand I wasn't eavesdropping—but I couldn't help overhearing scraps of your conversation with Matthew. You're not sailing tonight?

MIRANDA
No.

JOSIAH
Why?

MIRANDA
Sometimes you don't feel in the mood for ocean travel. I'm in one of those moods at the moment.

TOBY
How did he take the blow?

MIRANDA
He was sweet about it—understanding—of course. Said he'd come over here, if I needed him. I couldn't let him do that, naturally. It isn't *his* problem.

JOSIAH
          Steps up
What isn't?

MIRANDA

My own, personal—confusion.

JOSIAH

Looking at her

So you're confused, my daughter. Good! That means you're
normal. Have a glass of champagne.

*He pours the champagne and takes it to Miranda. She
looks him in the eye.*

MIRANDA

I told Matthew I would fly over next Friday.

JOSIAH

Oh?

As he hands her the glass

I'm afraid it's gone a little flat.

*He turns away, goes up to the table behind the sofa
and looks at a white geranium plant.*

Where did all the geraniums come from?

MIRANDA

I ordered them from that florist on Twelfth Street.

JOSIAH

You must have remembered I'm crazy about white geraniums.
All living, breathing plants. Leaf and branch, root and stem,
pushing up, pushing up.

He takes a gold cigarette case from his pocket.

JOSIAH

Toby, you've often admired this cigarette case—

TOBY

Sure have.

JOSIAH

I'd like you to have it.

TOBY
But listen, sir, I can't possibly.
> JOSIAH *hands it to him.*

JOSIAH
Think nothing of it.

TOBY
I'll think a great deal of it.
> JOSIAH *suddenly moves to the windows.*

JOSIAH
Who closed these curtains? Always—always let in the air! Curtains—walls—fences! Ceilings—roofs—clouds—thunderheads! Ceiling zero—subzero—grounded—grounded—
> *He yanks the curtain cord. The curtains swing open, but the long cord breaks and dangles from his hand.*

What! That damned thing is broken again. Where's Mrs. Malloy?

MIRANDA
Asleep, I expect.

JOSIAH
A little sleep, a little slumber, a little folding of the hands in sleep.
> *He calls into the garden.*

What did you say?
> *No reply is heard.*

TOBY
Nobody said a thing.

JOSIAH
> *He picks up a pair of long scissors from the desk, looks at them reflectively, then snips the brass weight from the end of the cord, advances to the center of the room, twisting the cord in his hands.*

When I was a boy there was a skipper of a fishing smack in
Georgian Bay who taught me sailor knots. I wonder do I still
remember?

He starts working deftly with the cord in his hands.
Look at Thankful, sitting there—so exquisitely innocent—so
unconfused—so hungry. A glass of milk, a ham on rye—and
thou. They are rare in this world, the true innocents—born
without original sin, I expect—at least without the sense of
guilt that rides the rest of us. Whatever their age, they never
grow old. They live and breathe youth, and impart it to others.
They are the life-givers.—This is called a bowline-on-a-bight,
Thankful.

Unties the knot and begins on another.
Did I ever tell you about Andy Farren? Great friend of mine—
First World War. Best flier I ever saw. He shot down twenty-two
German planes—he was absolutely devastating in combat. But
he couldn't stand the thought of going home after the Armistice
—he couldn't stand the prospect of going "back to normalcy."
So one day he headed his airplane for the open sea and flew on
and on until all his petrol was gone and he was never seen again.
You'd have understood if you'd known him. He was an innocent. He belonged in an earlier century. He was an anachronism.
He was a romantic—it was his heroics that finally brought him
down. Now I know why I felt so oddly relieved when I knew
he was dead—

MIRANDA
Relieved!

JOSIAH
Exactly—and not ashamed of it! One must belong to his times:
live them, write them, paint them, be of them: he never did,
never was. All he could do was to dwell in the past, enraged at
the present, full of fear of the future. Poor boy—poor old man

—but I'm glad he died when he did, as he did, with a gesture.

He looks at the new knot in his hands.

Whereas *this* one—now what kind of a sailor's knot would you call *that*?

TOBY

A hangman's noose?

JOSIAH

That shows how much you know about the sea—or about death.

He breaks the knot with a flick and throws the cord on the desk.

MIRANDA

To THANKFUL

Thanks, are you all packed?

THANKFUL

Just a few things I've got to throw—

She has started to go out.

JOSIAH

Wait! I have an announcement. I've made a discovery. As follows: the man who said of youth that no one knows its value until he's too old to enjoy it—that man was wrong! The great, the astonishing thing about it is that it may be enjoyed twice! Once, through one's own youth—and later, and better—through that of another. So—let's turn somersaults, let's swim out to the raft, let's go crabbing, let's have an ice-cream soda; the hermit has emerged from his cave, the monk from his cell; in brief, and to wit, I have found a girl—living, breathing, laughing, loving,—and my own.

He reaches for THANKFUL's *hand, draws her beside him.*

Yes, my darling—?

THANKFUL
> *Uncomprehending but delighted*

Why—yes . . . Why—of course.

MIRANDA
Go on, Thankful.

JOSIAH
> *To* THANKFUL

As soon as you get back from your trip to England—
> THANKFUL *looks bewildered*

I'll count the seconds 'til your return.

THANKFUL
> *To* MIRANDA

You know he *is* kind of—overwhelming. But terribly.

JOSIAH
There! You see how you've all been underrating me?

MIRANDA
> *To* THANKFUL

I'll be right up and help you, Thanks.

THANKFUL
And not even Sunday. Not even rainy.
> *She goes.*

JOSIAH
Why do you look so disapproving, Miranda? Surely you're not
thinking that there's a certain disparity in our ages?

MIRANDA
You needn't throw that in my teeth.

JOSIAH
And—surely you wouldn't deny me this—one, last fling?

MIRANDA

Or that either. Look here, Father. In the last twenty-four hours you've taught me to expect the incredible. But I never dreamt that you'd try to pull on us anything as crude and amateurish as this.

JOSIAH

Was I crude—heavy-handed—in my romantic approach?

MIRANDA

Oh, no—you can still charm a bird off a tree—and you know it.

JOSIAH

Ha! That's very apt—a bird—Thankful—a little bird. A lark! But I didn't exactly charm her down. I had to go out on a limb. And there she was—Thankful—a little lark—for awakening! Don't worry, Miranda. I've made more than my share of awful mistakes—and you know that better than anyone—but please remember, even a stopped clock is right twice a day.

> MIRANDA *gives him a searching look and goes.*
> JOSIAH *turns to* TOBY.

Do you happen to know why she decided to postpone?

TOBY

No, sir! I wasn't consulted.

JOSIAH

Could it be—she's found a new interest?

TOBY

Her father isn't new—except in certain respects.

JOSIAH

I wasn't referring to myself. To you.

TOBY

You think she might have looked twice at me?

JOSIAH

I had hoped.

TOBY

You're way off the beam. Take new bearings. She's going to marry Matthew Atwater if it's the last thing she does. Those were her very words.

JOSIAH

> *Turns away*

Then—I say—let her go.

> *He is now inwardly acknowledging total defeat.*

TOBY

And yourself with her?

JOSIAH

Why not? It's enough. It's more than enough. The assault—the constant assault—

TOBY

Lost the knack, again, have you?

JOSIAH

Knack? What knack?

TOBY

Of seeing the woods for the trees.

JOSIAH

Woods? What woods?

TOBY

Oh—life, say.

JOSIAH

Woods? You're right—a jungle! And you can have it. Anyone who wants it can.

TOBY
I'll take it, thanks.

JOSIAH
His voice rising
I tell you, it's a sell! If I didn't know it before, I know it now.
So the hell with it.
He turns on TOBY.
There's no reason for Miranda to change her plans. She's just
wasting her time around here.

TOBY
Angrily
I'm afraid we all are.

JOSIAH
Then tell her so. Tell her to get on that ship and go, carrying
with her no regrets. The British Customs are very severe with
people who try to smuggle in regrets.
He has sat down behind the desk.

TOBY
I have one or two things to tell *you*.

JOSIAH
Go ahead, my boy. Don't spare my feelings. I haven't any.

TOBY
To begin with, I'm damned glad my father's due back, so I'll
be clear of this case once and for all.

JOSIAH
I've been difficult, eh?

TOBY
They all are, the ones that won't co-operate. But this wins the
real first prize.

ACT TWO 121

JOSIAH
I enjoy excelling, even on a downgrade.

TOBY
And why are you trying to drag Miranda down with you?
JOSIAH *looks at him, sharply.*
You can't bear to let go of her, can you! So you're poisoning
her with your own despair.

JOSIAH
What are you talking about?

TOBY
I'm talking about your daughter, and the health of her heart
and mind. Whatever you do to yourself is your business, I'm
sorry to say. But what you do to Miranda—

JOSIAH
And is that *your* business?

TOBY
I wish it were. Then I could really do something about it.

JOSIAH
What would you do, Toby?

TOBY
I'd marry her tonight. I'd prove to her that she can be loved
for herself—and not merely as a sort of subdivision of Josiah
Bolton. You're asserting your domination more violently than
ever. You're giving her something terrible to remember you by.
You're making the attachment all the stronger, all the more
strangling.

JOSIAH
Attachment?

TOBY

That's the word. You're cooking up real tragedy for Miranda, permanent tragedy. She was trying to escape from it. Maybe she didn't choose the wisest means of escape. But she was trying. And she deserved your sympathy, your help, your pity. Instead of which—you're very skillfully fixing it so that there can be no escape for her, by any means, ever.

JOSIAH
    Quietly, coldly
Perhaps I'm out of date—but—is this the modern concept of correct professional behavior for a doctor?

TOBY

Luckily, I am not here on a professional basis.

JOSIAH

So you can say what you please—and so, by your leave, can I. My daughter is miserable because she is full of illusions about me. I have sought to shatter them by letting her see me as I really am—ruthless, callous. And that may give her a clearer view of Matthew Atwater.

TOBY

All very fine—very slick. But what you're *really* doing is shifting to her the responsibility for your own failure.
    MIRANDA *has come in on that last sentence.*

MIRANDA

Toby! What are you saying!

TOBY

I'm talking out of turn. But I've got to do it! The air's got to be cleared. It's suffocating!
    To JOSIAH
Of all the lowdown advantages to take of your own child, the threat you're making is the lowest I ever heard of.

MIRANDA

Have you gone crazy?

TOBY

No! Sane! I'm no psychiatrist—nor ever will be. I don't like the brain as a study. I prefer the digestive tract. It's much more orderly and efficient than the brain, and also much cleaner. But I'm a doctor and I've looked the gray rat in the eye quite a number of times, and always I've been given a fair chance to fight him off. But this is the most humiliating experience of my career so far—and the most contemptible—and I have to say so—and the hell with the ethics of my profession, the hell with the Hippocratic oath!

    JOSIAH *laughs.*

MIRANDA

That's brave talk, Toby—but you won't get anywhere with it.
    However, there is a note of tender admiration in her tone.

JOSIAH

I don't know—he just might.
    He rises.
Perhaps I can help you, Toby, by giving you a few homely truths about this Josiah Bolton. I've known the fellow for many years, but suddenly I have a new, and I think true, view of him —and I'll try to give it in *my* best professional manner.
    He crosses to front of the desk and continues to them both, in much the manner of a lawyer addressing judge and jury.
Have a look at him, ladies and gentlemen: a man who, from his youth was bitten and consumed by the desire to get on. Once he left, he never went back—to the town he was born in, the schools he attended, the college that graduated him. Desperately afraid of all human relationships and of his own and others'

emotions, he finally starved them out, scared them off—fearful, of course, that they might take from him something of himself. Vanity, vanity, saith the Preacher—

MIRANDA
It's not true! You're the most—
          JOSIAH *bangs on the desk.*

JOSIAH
If you please, Madam! No heckling in the court!
          He goes on.
No one was allowed any part of this individual, but what he chose to give them—never more than his thoughts and words— tangy and pungent at times, perhaps, but still dried herring. He sought to, and eventually established complete residence in the realms of the mind: his only exchange with others rigidly intellectual, except perhaps in the case of his daughter—

MIRANDA
Yes!

JOSIAH
But that, only when she was quite young. Later, he deliberately allowed her to identify herself with him—fostered this relationship until they became almost as one person.

MIRANDA
Toby—stop him!

TOBY
No!

JOSIAH
Then when the cruel, inevitable necessity came to break the bond, he stupidly wondered at the fact that, from the vacuum in which he left her, she went on to another, perhaps less

benevolent despot, and quite as suave, ruthless and cynical as he
—and two years older

He looks straight at her

—than I am!

MIRANDA

It's not so—it's not that way at all!

JOSIAH

Unhappily, it is. If Josiah Bolton had not been in her life what
he was, there'd have been no Matthew Atwater, or anything
like him now.

MIRANDA

Liar—liar—

JOSIAH

But there it was. So when he'd finally cut off everyone around
him and at last stood alone, as he thought he'd always wished
to, he—imagine what!—he found himself lonely with the bleak,
cold, crushing loneliness of the truly prideful ones: the simple
capacity for friendship gone, the human capacity for affection,
finally even the grim capacity for self-satisfaction—And serves
him right!

MIRANDA

I tell you I won't have it that way!

JOSIAH

Why not?—Not the world or his times to blame for it, mind
you—himself, and himself only. Arrived at last! Himself destroyed and his daughter set by him firmly on the path to the
same end. A fine, crowning achievement to a lifelong struggle.
What do you say? Hm-m? *I* say, let him rot!—Go on—clear
out now, both of you. Leave me alone.

MIRANDA

No! We'll not! We'll never!

JOSIAH

Don't be fearful any more, daughter. Something else goes in the process: courage. I'm likely to hang on for years. So while we're facing it squarely at last, let's agree there's been a mistake made, shall we? And the accidents purely accidental. What do you say? All willing?

MIRANDA

No, No! You're handing me some dirty old wool to pull over my own eyes so that I'll stop seeing what's plain as day and I'll tell you, "Go on, Father dear, go on out to Arizona and have another try."

JOSIAH

Try?

MIRANDA

Answer me this, Father, for God's sake—who is it but yourself that you want to hurt?

JOSIAH

Nobody. You can believe that.

MIRANDA

Then on whose doorstep do you plan to leave the body?

JOSIAH

That question is irrelevant, immaterial—

TOBY

It's right on the button—that's where it is. Maybe you thought you were kidding when you talked about a second threshold. Maybe there *is* one leading into a new life, not death. And maybe you haven't got the guts to step across.

MIRANDA

How dare you talk to my father like that? He isn't afraid of anything. He's a great man and he's done great work. He's

made his own way since the beginning. Everyone close to him
has let him down. And life's piled up on him to a point where
it's—it's insupportable.
>   *She goes to* JOSIAH.
Father, you can do what you like with your life. It's all yours.
But I'm telling you now: you do *that* with it and I'll do the
same with my own, and straight off! And that's a promise!

TOBY
Mandy!

JOSIAH
>   *Greatly shocked*
That threat is not worthy of you.

MIRANDA
>   *Tears in her eyes*
It's no threat—believe me—it's a promise!
>   TOBY *has gone close to* MIRANDA.

TOBY
Mandy! Let's not hear any more of that.

MIRANDA
>   *To* TOBY
Oh, I wouldn't want to—I wouldn't want to at all. Because—
for all the awful things about it and all the jams I get into, I
love living, I love it—and—
>   *To* JOSIAH
—oh, if only *you* would again—because I love you too—and I
couldn't stand to see you go that way, and me not having been
able to—and I'm so crazy about Toby that I don't know where
I'm at and—
>   *Suddenly she stops, looks appalled, turns to* TOBY.
What did I say just then?

JOSIAH

I believe you said that you are—

MIRANDA

She swings back to Josiah.
All the same, I'd do it! I would, I would! I promise, promise, promise! Hear me?

JOSIAH

I hear you.

MIRANDA

Then—what—what have you to say?

JOSIAH

What do you want me to do?

MIRANDA

What we've been asking you—begging you—get yourself well.

JOSIAH

I'll do anything. Anything you wish.

MIRANDA

Looking at him, searching him
Do you mean that? Is that the truth?

JOSIAH

For as far as I can see, I mean it. . . . And—what you said about Toby—did you mean *that*, too?

MIRANDA

I—yes—
She casts a sidelong, embarrassed glance at Toby.
—I guess so. I guess I'm not responsible for my emotions these days.

JOSIAH

Then what are you going to do about it?

THANKFUL *comes in.*

THANKFUL

Oh, dear—I hate to say it—I love this place so—I've had such an ecstatic time—

JOSIAH

What are you going to do about it?

MIRANDA

To JOSIAH

I don't know.

THANKFUL

Pause

I—I hate to be interrupting—but, honestly, I think I've got to be—

JOSIAH

Ah yes—the time has come, delicious. You have new continents to conquer. So—*bon voyage*, Thankful! Goodbye!

MIRANDA *turns away, wanting to think this out, to adjust herself to these new circumstances.* TOBY *watches her.*

THANKFUL

But aren't you coming to the boat?

JOSIAH

Certainly not! The most depressing kind of farewell. Crowds— orchids—"What an attractive cabin! What a motherly stewardess! Whoever sent that gorgeous basket of apricots! Well— there goes the gong. All ashore that's going ashore! Guess I

might as well be getting off now." Goodbye, Thankful. Good
luck.

> *He kisses her lightly on the brow.*

Blessings from your devoted grandfather.

THANKFUL
> *Turning to* TOBY

Well! You certainly never know where you stand with that one.
> *She starts to go.*

Goodbye, Miranda, sweetie.

MIRANDA
Wait—Thankful, I'm going with you.
> *She turns to* JOSIAH.

I'm going to sail.

THANKFUL
Miranda!

MIRANDA
Toby—you realize—you must—that I have to go over and explain it myself? That no cables, letters, telephones will do? You
realize—

TOBY
Being you, yes. But—I'd like to see you off.
> *Pause*

THANKFUL
Then let's go—

TOBY
I'll get a taxi. May I come back later, sir?

JOSIAH
Of course. I'll be up.

> TOBY *goes with* THANKFUL. *After a moment,* JOSIAH
> *turns to* MIRANDA.

JOSIAH
No sentiment between us. Never was any.

MIRANDA
No.

JOSIAH
So I can say something, can't I?

MIRANDA
If you want to.

JOSIAH
I'm glad about what's happened today.

MIRANDA
Because you discovered I'm not such a brain, after all—I'm just plain dumb.
>   *He crosses to* MIRANDA.

JOSIAH
I discovered that my daughter doesn't want her father to die.
>   *She looks at him, quickly, gratefully. He gives her a*
>   *brusque little kiss.*
Now—get the hell out of here. Go on. Don't keep the Cunard Line waiting.

MIRANDA
>   *Happily*
I'll fly back. What I have to do in London won't take ten minutes. You know Matthew.

JOSIAH
I know Matthew.

MIRANDA
And you know me.

JOSIAH
Smiles
Yes, Miranda. At last!
> *She gives him a radiant look, and a gay little wave, and goes.* JOSIAH *stands still for a while, then goes slowly to the window and looks down into the garden.* MALLOY *appears and picks up the tray from the coffee table.*

JOSIAH
Get yourself to bed, Malloy.

MALLOY
And you, sir?

JOSIAH
Presently . . .
> *He is looking into the garden.*
Oh—Malloy—I want you to have somebody in tomorrow—a carpenter, or somebody. I want to have these steps fixed. They're rickety. We mustn't have any accidents.

MALLOY
Yes, sir. Good night, sir.

JOSIAH
Good night, Malloy.
> MALLOY *has gone out. As* JOSIAH *looks down, he seems to be listening. Suddenly he speaks*
Yes—I hear you all right. And I have to tell you that I'm not interested. So go away. I don't want you around here. Go away. Beat it. Get out!
> *He turns away from the window.*

CURTAIN